UNIVERSA

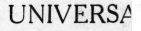

SELECTED A

SANSKRIT RELIGIOUS LITERATURE

BY

SWAMI YATISWARANANDA

SRI RAMAKRISHNA MATH
MYLAPORE MADRAS 600 004

Published by
Adhyaksha
Sri Ramakrishna Math
Mylapore, Chennai-4

XIV-2M 5C-1-2010
ISBN 81-7120-511-9

Printed in India at
Sri Ramakrishna Math Printing Press
Mylapore, Chennai-4

CONTENTS

CONTENTS

INTRODUCTION

अनादिनिधनं विष्णुं सर्वलोकमहेश्वरम् ।
लोकाध्यक्षं स्तुवन्नित्यं सर्वदुःखातिगो भवेत् ॥

*" By always praising the all-pervading
Being, who is without beginning and without
end, who is the supreme Lord of all the
worlds, and who is the eternal controller of
the universe, one gets beyond all grief."*

THIS book containing choice prayers from
select hymns presents to the devotee just a
little cream of devotion from the mighty milk
ocean of Sanskrit religious literature. The
lines are free from sectarian bias and speak
of the universal aspect of the Deity common
to all religions and creeds. As such, they are
sure to appeal to all seekers after Truth who
follow the path of devotion in some form or

other, and want passages for meditation, praise and prayer all together.

THE USE OF HYMNS AND PRAYERS

Of the threefold forms of worship—physical, verbal and mental, that is, external adoration, invocation by praises and prayers, and meditation—the first, consisting of rituals and ceremonials of the past, has almost fallen out of use in the life of the individual, and this is greatly due to the stress of activity and lack of leisure and other conveniences in modern life. Noticing the tendency of the age, the authors of the Puranas—the popular scriptures—have laid great emphasis on verbal and mental worship, and of these, again, particularly on verbal worship, as it is easier to practise than the other. " The seeker after Truth," says Manu, " reaches the highest goal by Japa only ". And " Japa," declares the Mahabharata, " is said to be the best of all spiritual practices." The Vishnu Purana supports this view whole-heartedly when it observes, " That which one obtained through meditation in the Satya Yuga (the Golden Age), through sacrifice in the Treta Yuga (Silver Age), and through worship in the Dvapara Yuga (Brazen Age), may be achieved in the Kali Yuga (Iron Age) by reciting the names of the Lord." And this recitation of the divine names, or Japa, implies also dwelling on the divine attributes. Sometimes it may mean reciting only one name and one attribute, and sometimes many names and many attributes. The former is usually called Japa and the latter Stotra, but generally the two are bracketed together.

THE PLACE OF HYMNS AND PRAYERS IN WORSHIP

Sound and thought are inseparably connected, the former being an expression or vehicle of the latter. The spiritual aspirant

takes the help of the sound symbol with a
view to awaken the holy thought in his
mind. On rising to the mental plane he may
do away with the sound symbol altogether.
And if he is able to ascend to the heights of
realisation and lose himself in divine communion, he dispenses with the mental worship even. But until the divine vision dawns
on him, he has to seek the help of symbols—
material, verbal or mental—which may be
taken up either singly or jointly. " Material
worship (or the use of an image as symbol-
ising the ideal)," say the Hindu scriptures,
" is the first step ; then comes the repetition
of the Lord's name and the singing of His
praise ; the next course is mental worship or
meditation ; and the final stage is the realisation of the One without a second." Thus
man comes to take up higher and higher
forms of spiritual practice in his march
towards the highest illumination. And in
this matter hymns and prayers have ever
formed an important aid.

VARIOUS TYPES OF WORSHIPPERS

In all ages and in all religions, the spiritual aspirants and devotees have given natural expression to their innermost yearnings and noblest sentiments in hymns, psalms, praises and prayers. Sometimes they sing and pray out of the fullness of their hearts, dwelling in exalted moods untouched by cares and wants. But in most cases it is a consciousness of limitations and imperfections, or the sense of misery and helplessness that makes the weary and struggling souls turn to the omnipotent and ever-perfect Being for solace and succour. As Sri Krishna says in the Bhagavad Gita, four kinds of persons worship God,—the distressed, the seeker of knowledge, the seeker of enjoyment, and the wise. It is natural for the man of spiritual illumination to worship God, to meditate on Him and to speak of His glory out of his overflowing love and devotion. But the case of the others is

different. Buffetted by the troubles of life
or worried by the consciousness of sin, and
realising the uselessness of human aid, the
care-worn soul turns to the Divine for safety
and protection. The seeker of enjoyments,
finding all human efforts fruitless, looks up
in his helplessness to God for the fulfilment
of his desires. The seeker of knowledge
may not have any worldly trouble or material
desires to disturb him, but he feels in his
heart of hearts a soul-hunger, a sense of void
or the misery of a limited existence that nothing in the world can remove. His soul
yearns for the higher life and in the course
of his search he comes to God, the source of
peace and blessedness. It is out of dire
necessity that all these types of devotees
seek the divine help and grace. Thus to
them God is a constitutional necessity. And
so great is this need that even sceptics in
their helplessness and despair have been
heard to cry out to the Almighty for solace
and support. The so-called agnostic's prayer

—" O God, if there be a God, save my soul,
if I have a soul "—however humorous it
may sound at first, contains a deep truth
that cannot but be recognised by the sym-
pathetic student of religious psychology.

THE ONE AND THE MANY IN THE VEDAS

This great truth we find throughout our
survey of the different epochs of Hindu
civilisation. Worshippers and devotees in
India have all along sent forth supplications
and thanksgivings, praises and prayers, to
the Almighty from the very depths of their
being. The Rig Veda and other Samhitas
—the oldest religious literature of India,
nay, of the whole world—are nothing but
collections of hymns sung mostly in praise
of the deities, Indra, Mitra, Varuna, Agni
and others. Indra is described as the
thunderer and giver of rains, as the ' king of
all that is fixed and moving ', ' before whom
both heaven and earth go down '. Mitra is

spoken of as the god who regulates the course of the sun, and is intimately associated with Varuna who dwells in the bright blue sky, who is merciful to the penitent and releases them from sin. Agni is the god in the fire, ' an immortal who has taken up his abode among mortals ', the deity through whom all other gods receive oblations and worship. He is often described as the father (Universal Prayers, No. 12) and also as brother, kinsman and friend. Pushan was the deity representing the beneficent power of the sun and the giver of prosperity and protection (Universal Prayers, No. 13). Savita was also the solar deity who stimulated life and activity in the world (invoked in the well-known Gayatri Mantra—Universal Prayers, No. 14.) There are many other names of gods occurring in the Vedic hymns. And it is a very striking fact that at the very dawn of man's spiritual consciousness the Vedic seers, while they prayed mostly for their material welfare and happiness,

could recognise the existence of an indwelling
Spirit at the back of each natural phenomenon, and some of them went so far as to
realise the one God at the back of the many
gods. Behind the apparently polytheistic
conceptions there is almost everywhere a
deeply engrained monotheism that is clearly
expressed as each god is invoked and worshipped as omnipotent, omniscient and even
omnipresent. Indeed, many of these seers,
especially the most advanced ones, worshipped the one and the same divine Being in
His various manifestations. This is made
clear in the famous Rig Vedic hymn
(I, 164, 46) in which the Rishi, in his praise
of Surya—the most concrete of the solar
gods—goes so far as to declare : " They call
Him Indra, Mitra, Varuna and Agni. The
Being is one, but sages call Him variously."
And this wonderful current of applied monotheism has been flowing on in the hearts of
the Hindu devotees with unabted, nay,
increasing strength up to the present day.

THE IMPERSONAL

In their search after Truth, the Vedic seers came face to face with the one supreme Deity, ' who has become all this ' (Rig Veda, VIII, 58, 2), ' whom the learned and the wise describe in many forms of expressions ' (Rig Veda, X, 114, 5). This is monotheism pure and simple. But the bold seers of ancient India made a further advance, and rising above the idea of a personal, nay, even a cosmic Deity, they came to realise also the impersonal Being who is spoken of in neuter terms—a glimpse of whom we get in the Nasadiya Sukta (Rig Veda X, 129) : " There was then neither what is, nor what is not. There was no sky, nor the heaven which is beyond. . . . Then death was not, nor immortality ; there was no difference of day and night. That One breathed, breathless in Itself. It existed but without exerting or manifesting Itself, and there was nothing other than It." Herein we find the germ of pure monism that has been so clearly and frequently expressed in the Upanishads and later scriptures.

THE PERSONAL AND THE IMPERSONAL

As already pointed out, the idea of the one supreme God who is exalted above all gods has been an abiding fact in the religious consciousness of the Hindu. But so far as names of gods are concerned, there has taken place a great revolution. Names like Vishnu and Rudra that were of minor importance came to be very prominent in later times, while those like Indra, Mitra and Varuna were practically forgotten and replaced by other divine names. The trinity of Brahmā, Vishnu and Shiva came to occupy a most important place in the thought and literature of the land. Brahmā represents the aspect of creation, Vishnu the aspect of preservation, and Shiva the aspect of dissolution. These three aspects are connected

with the three stages through which the entire universe, including both the macrocosm
and the microcosm, has inevitably got to
pass. The trinity are the three aspects of
the same Brahman associated with Maya or
Prakriti (creative Power or primal Nature)
consisting of the Gunas[1]—the primordial
modes of Energy known as Sattva, Rajas
and Tamas—which evolve into ego, mind,
senses, bodies and sense-objects. Sattva
implies purity and knowledge ; Rajas, passion and restless activity ; Tamas, ignorance
and indolence. This perception of the unity
of Being and Power at the back of all stages
of evolution is not quite possible for the
undeveloped mind, but it was fully recognised by the seers of the Upanishads when they
declared : " That out of which all beings are
born, by which they are sustained after birth,
into which they enter at the time of dissolution—seek to know That. That is
Brahman."

[1] See Introduction to the " Divine Life," pp. 24 etc.

In later Hinduism, besides the adoration of the trinity, the worship of Rama and Krishna, both Incarnations of Vishnu, and also the worship of Shakti, the divine Mother-power, came to be prevalent everywhere. But in the midst of these phenomenal changes, the Hindu's conception of the highest Deity, his spiritual hopes and aspirations, his seeking the divine aid and guidance, his hunger for spiritual communion, have all remained unchanged. And with the march of time it has been recognised more and more that the Impersonal or the Supra-personal—the Nirguna Brahman transcending all Power and attributes—is the background of the Saguna Brahman or Brahman in combination with Power and attributes, that It is the Reality behind the Personal and all personalities, and that although the manifestations might differ, the Unmanifest ever remains the same. There are sectarians who might speak of the superiority of the particular gods,

incarnations and prophets, but seers having
the totality of vision have regarded all personalities, either of gods or god-men, to be
diverse expressions of the Impersonal and the
Supreme, which, like the ocean, may give
rise to innumerable waves but continues to
be infinite and unfathomable as ever. Indeed, men of the highest spiritual illumination have realised that whatever may be the
holy Personality one may begin with, the
goal of spiritual life lies in the experience of
the Impersonal—the One without a second,
in which the worshipper and the worshipped,
nay, God, souls and the universe get merged
and become one and indivisible.

DIFFERENT CONCEPTIONS
OF THE DEITY

In our study of the hymns and prayers
we come across various conceptions of God.
Some devotees think of Him as possessing
both Divine forms and attributes. Others

speak of Him as having no forms but being endowed with the noblest qualities. Others, again, while they take note of the Personal, stress the Impersonal of which the former is regarded as a manifestation. And sometimes we find that all these ideas are more or less combined. But usually the devotees worship and pray to the Divine through a particular manifestation or form which serves as a prop for supporting their faith and devotion. Indeed, the commonalty cannot help associating human forms and human attributes with the Deity. But the comparatively advanced souls, however, who have clarified their understanding and have risen to a higher conception of the Divinity, speak of the one Deity 'who is in the fire, who is in the water, who has pervaded the whole universe' (Universal Prayers, N. 40), who, though One without a second and formless, produces various forms (Universal Prayers, No. 42), who has become man and woman, youth and maiden, and is born in manifold forms (Universal Prayers, No. 43). As is well expressed in the Kena Upanishad, " He is the ear of the ear, the mind of the mind, the speech of the speech, the cosmic Power at the back of the vital energy." God is the immanent Principle. He is not merely the God of gods but is also the Self of all, the life universal (Universal Prayers No. 49 *et seq.*). Proceeding further in the spiritual path, the seer realises the Transcendental who is ' beyond speech and thought ' —who is "invisible, unrelated, unperceivable, devoid of all connotations, unthinkable, indefinable, essentially of the nature of Self-consciousness alone, negation of all relative existence, peace, supreme bliss, and the One without a second " (Mandukyopanishad).

WORSHIP OF THE PERSONAL-IMPERSONAL : ILLUSTRATIONS

The worship of the divine Personality or the incarnated Principle has certainly an unquestionable place in spiritual life ; it is indispensable for most devotees. As Sri Krishna declares in the Bhagavad Gita, the path of the Absolute and the unmanifest is very hard to follow. Hence we find that in all religious faiths the devotee worships the Lord, resigning all his actions to Him, meditating on Him with devotion and concentration, and regarding Him as the supreme goal of life— a fact recognised by the Upanishadic seers when they pray : " Desirous of emancipation, I seek refuge in that effulgent Being whose light reveals the knowledge of the Atman, who first creates the cosmic Soul and delivers to him the supreme knowledge, who is without parts, without action, tranquil, without fault, without taint, who is the supreme bridge to immortality " (Universal Prayers, Nos. 46—48).

The Impersonal is beyond the reach of the devotee, while the personal does not satisfy his philosophic sense. Hence the whorship of the Personal-Impersonal has been

most popular in all higher forms of spiritual
practice. And this is true of the worshippers
of Krishna or Rama, Shiva or Vishnu, gods
or goddesses. In the course of his prayer
the devotee of Krishna sings in the Bhagavad
Gita : " Salutations to Thee before and to
Thee behind. Salutations to Thee on every
side. O Lord, Thou art everything. Infinite
in power and infinite in prowess, Thou pervadest all. Therefore Thou art the all "
(Universal Prayers, No. 57). The worshipper
of Rama also declares in Valmiki Ramayana : " Thou art manifest in all creatures,
in the animal as well as in the holy man.
Thou art manifest in all directions, in the
sky as well as in rivers and mountains "
(Universal Prayers, No. 75). The devotee of
Shiva also sings in the same strain in the
Skanda Purana : " O Lord, Thou art the
one Brahman without a second. Thou art
everything. Thou art the one Truth, and
verily there is nothing but Thee. O Thou
destroyer of misery, Thou alone dost exist

eternally and none besides. Therefore I take
refuge in Thee, the great Lord " (Universal
Prayers, No. 120). The devotee of Vishnu
also gives expression to the same idea when
he prays in the Vishnu Purana : " Lord,
Thou abidest in all ; Thou art all ; Thou assumest all forms ; Thou art the origin of all.
Thou art the soul of all. Salutations unto
Thee " (Universal Prayers, No. 120). The
worshipper of the divine Mother also sees
the same immanent and transcendent Being
in Her when he sings Her praise in the Mar-
kandeya Purana : " Thou art the cause of all
the worlds. Thou art the embodiment of
three Gunas ; yet Thou art known to be
transcendental and faultless. Incomprehensible Thou art even to the greatest of the
gods. Thou art the refuge of all. The whole
world is but a part of Thee. Thou art the
unmanifest, primordial, supreme creatress "
(Universal Prayers, No. 149). To the enlightened worshipper the Mother is no other
than Brahman. And addressing Her the

devotee says in the Mahakala Samhita:
"Thou hast neither name nor lineage; neither
birth nor death; neither abode nor activity.
Thou hast neither pain nor pleasure; neither
friend nor enemy; neither bondage nor
freedom. Thou art the One without a second,
known as the Brahman supreme" (Universal Prayers, No. 205).

Thus the conception of the Personal-Impersonal of the One in the many, permeates
the entire Hindu religious consciousness—a
fact that will be clearly understood by those
who are able to enter into the true spirit of
the Hindu scriptures.

HIGHER CONCEPTION OF GOD—
CONSCIOUSNESS OF SIN

But it is the advanced seers of Truth who
can speak from experience of the Immanent
and the Transcendent with whom they associ-
ate the idea of absolute purity and holiness. The undeveloped worshipper, however,

cannot really entertain any exalted conception of the Godhead. Even if he professes to believe in the all-pervading Spirit, he conceives of Him as an omnipotent being possessing human form and human feelings. Even if he considers his God to be all-loving towards the devotees, he holds Him to be also jealous and fearful, ever ready to punish His devotee's enemies and condemn the 'unbeliever' to eternal hell. Not unoften does the devout worshipper sing in the name of his God of love a veritable hymn of hate. Further he sees real and imaginary evils in others but is unconscious of much greater evils that are to be found in himself. This is a phenomenon witnessed in all religions and creeds more or less in all parts of the world. But as the aspirant outgrows his primitive ideas, he comes to cherish a nobler conception of God, who is not only omnipresent but also the source of all purity and perfection. Further, he also comes to possess greater and greater introspection with reference to himself, and this is in reality a chief mark of his spiritual progress. With the dawn of the inner vision the devotee is able to detect easily the evils and impurities that taint his body and mind. He is tormented by a sense of sin and imperfection, and these he wants to shed through the grace and touch of God—the great purifier—who, according to the Upanishadic seers, is all-pervading, self-resplendent, formless, pure and untarnished by evil, who is ' free from sin ', ' who dwells in the sinless heart ' and who ' cannot be realised by one who has not turned away from wickedness and has not controlled his mind and senses '

GOD THE PURIFIER AND SAVIOUR

Indeed, this conception of God, the ever-pure and the purifier, is also found in the Rig Veda Samhita itself, in which the Rishi prays to Varuna, the great moral ruler of the universe, for being saved from the bonds of sin and evil (Rig Veda, I, 25 ; II, 82 etc.), for forgiveness from sin,— a thought that occurs time and again in the mass of Vedic and other Hindu religious literature. In the Taittiriya Aranyaka the Rishi prays : "Being purified by the holy, all-pervading and eternal presence of the effulgent Being, man gets rid of evil. May we, too, go beyond the touch of sin, our great enemy, being freed from impurity by that ever-holy presence that purifies all" (Universal Prayers, No. 33). Purity being the condition for receiving divine grace and attaining spiritual illumination and freedom, the devotee prays : " Whatever sins have been committed by me, by thought, word or deed—may the supreme Lord, the source of strength, wisdom and purity. forgive me and cleanse me of them all " (Universal Prayers, No. 31). Indeed, it is a constant prayer of the devotee in the Upanishads : " May He, the creator and lord of all, the supporter of gods, . . . endow us with good thoughts " (Universal

Prayers, No. 41). For evil and impurity
in any form cause the greatest misery
to the sincere seeker, as they stand in
the way of his union with the Divine.
Hence in his distress he turns again and
again to the Lord, the sanctifier and saviour.
And the Lord also in His infinite mercy
speaks to him the words of hope: " Even if
Thou art the most sinful among all the sinful, yet by the raft of divine knowledge thou
shalt cross sin " (Bhagavad Gita, IV, 36).
And the God of love comforts the devotee
and asks him thus to surrender himself to
Him : " Relinquish the path of formal religion and take refuge in me. I will liberate
thee from all sins. Grieve not " (Bhagavad
Gita, XVIII, 66). Indeed, the idea of purity
and holiness along with that of mercy and
compassion is so inseparably connected with
the conception of God in Hinduism that it is
accepted as an axiomatic truth. And from
the depths of the devotee's heart rise the
prayers : " Do Thou forgive me, O Lord,

for all my sins. . . . Glory unto Thee,
Thou ocean of mercy " (Universal Prayers,
No. 229) ; and " I have committed a thousand
faults and am fallen into the terrible ocean
of births and deaths. O Thou saviour,
being helpless, I have taken refuge in Thee.
Be pleased to make me Thine own " (Universal Prayers, No. 252).

The Depths of Hindu Religion
of Love

Consciousness of sin and trust in God's
forgiveness are certainly essential for man's
spiritual growth at a certain stage of his
evolution. But these are not the dominating
ideas in higher Hinduism, as all Hindu sects
and creeds believe in the potential divinity
and the purity not merely of God but also of
the true Self of man, as much as in its innate
freedom from all limitations. The heart of
the Hindu devotee yearns more for divine
love and communion and spiritual freedom

than for anything else. He stresses the
personal aspect of the Personal-Impersonal.
He wants to come into living touch with
Him, to enter into personal relationship with
Him. And in his attempt to realise his goal,
he gives expression to a variety of sentiments
and attitudes, the depths of which cannot
be easily gauged by a superficial observer.
God, according to him, is not only the
author of the universe, the all-pervading
cause of all that exists, but He is to him
specially the God of love who manifests His
divine glory in intimate relationship with
the devotee as father, mother, master, friend
and child. He manifests even as the eternal
lover of the human soul that yearns from
the depths of its being for union with the
Beloved. This yearning is what is called
divine love, and according to Narada, it is
' ineffable ' and implies ' the consecration of
all activities to God ' and ' a feeling of
anguish when His presence is forgotten '.
Ordinarily the devotees worship Him as the

divine master, father or mother ; the eternal lover is beyond their reach. But still there are some blessed souls who are fit to approach Him with an all-consuming and all-embracing love that includes all the other attitudes in its sweep, and in which these find their highest fulfilment and realisation. Very touching is the prayer that rises forth from the heart of Sri Yamunacharya : " O Lord, first of all do Thou hear my prayer. I am speaking only the truth and not falsehood. Unless Thou bestowest Thy mercy on me, Thou will never get one more deserving than myself " (Universal Prayers, No. 259). " Thou art the father, the mother, the husband and the son. Thou art the dear friend, the relative, the teacher and the goal of the universe. I am Thine own, Thy servant and attendant ; Thou art my only refuge. I have taken shelter in Thee, and verily, O Lord, does my burden rest wholly on Thee " (Universal Prayers, No. 263). With an unsurpassed

passionate love does Sri Chaitanya also pray
to his Beloved : " O Lord of the universe, I
want neither wealth nor attendants, neither
a charming wife nor intellectual attainments.
Do Thou grant that I may be blessed in
every birth with the selfless devotion to Thee,
O Lord " (Universal Prayers, No. 266).

THE ALL-EMBRACING RANGE
OF HINDU SPIRITUAL EXPERIENCE

The deep raptures of ecstatic love are
soul- enthralling. But these do not exhaust
the spiritual experience of the Hindu
devotee. There are souls of extraordinary
spiritual calibre who want to encompass
within the range of their experience both the
Personal and the Impersonal. Their spiritual
consciousness refuses to be limited and
circumscribed. They take up all attitudes,
they realise all divine manifestations. They
enjoy the Beloved in manifold ways. But at
times a burning hunger for the Infinite seizes

their souls. They dive into the depths of the Absolute and lose themselves in transcendental Existence, Knowledge and Bliss. And when they come back to the plane of relative existence, they see everything reflecting the radiance of the Infinite, in whom ' the sun shines not, nor the moon and the stars, nor the lightning, much less fire ', but by whose light everything is lighted. Realising the Transcendent in the Immanent, the eternal Principle in all personalities, the One in the many, they love all, they worship all, they enjoy all. They are quite at home with the Absolute as with the Relative. A glimpse of this all-encompassing spiritual vision we get in the hymns and praises composed by Sri Sankaracharya, the great monistic philosopher and psalmist. He sees the one Reality at the back of everything as in his own soul. He meditates on It and realises that he is no other than Brahman. " At dawn I meditate within my heart on the self-effulgent Atman, the existence-knowledge-bliss

3

Absolute, the goal of the highest ascetics, the
Transcendental and the Eternal, who is beyond the states of waking, dream and sleep.
I am verily that indivisible Brahman and not
a combination of material elements " (Universal Prayers, No. 226).

THE ONE WORSHIPPED IN MANY
FORMS

Sankara, the true seer, recognises the same
divine Principle in all divine ideals. He
offers his salutations to the Guru in whom
also he sees the same eternal and infinite
Being : " I offer my salutations to that beneficent Being who is incarnate as the Guru.
He, the Atman, appearing as the individual
soul through the power of Maya, sees (in
the waking state)—as one does in sleep—the
universe, which in reality exists within
Himself, as something external, like a city
seen reflected in a mirror. But in His enlightened state He realises His own Self,

the One without a second" (Universal Prayers, No. 223).

To Sankara, Shiva, Vishnu and all gods and goddesses speak of the same Infinite, which gives the true meaning to the finite. Addressing Shiva he says : " I adore the Lord, the supreme Atman, the One, the primordial seed of the universe, the desireless and the formless, who is realised through the symbol Om, from whom the universe comes into being, by whom it is sustained, and into whom it dissolves" (Universal Prayers, No. 225).

With a deep feeling of devotion he prays to Vishnu : " O Thou Lord all-pervading, do Thou remove my egotism, and calm my mind. Do Thou take away from me the illusion of the world. Do Thou increase my love for all beings, and save me from the ocean of worldly existence." He continues : " It is the waves that merge themselves in the ocean, and not the ocean in the waves. So, verily, O Lord, when all differences are removed, it is I that become absorbed in Thee, and not Thou in me" (Universal Prayers, Nos. 237, 238).

The heart of the great monistic philosopher responds most tenderly to the call of the Mother's love, and placing himself in the position of the ordinary devotee, most touchingly he says : " O Mother, in this world, in the midst of Thy numerous worthy sons, I happen to be a rare specimen of wantonness. Yet, O Thou beneficent one, it is not proper for Thee to have abandoned me, Thy child. For, a bad son may sometimes be born but never has there been a bad mother " (Universal Prayers, No. 248).

And Mother to him is the only refuge : " O Mother, I have made no charity ; I have done no meditation ; I have observed no rituals ; nor have I uttered any prayer or holy name. I have performed no worship ; nor have I purified myself through proper invocations. Therefore, O Thou Mother of the universe, Thou art my only refuge ;

Thou art my only refuge " (Universal Prayers,
No. 240). But to him, in spite of the
wonderful play of the tenderest sentiments,
the Divine Mother is no other than Brahman
and human personality is only Her reflection.
She out of sport has divided the one absolute
Intelligence into God and souls. And it is
in Her being that he wants to lose himself:
" O Mother of the universe, when will my
senses become controlled ? When shall I
have neither enemies nor friends ? When
shall I be completely free from false and
deluding hopes ? When will my false mind
be destroyed with its roots ? " (Universal
Prayers, No. 243).

Indeed, when we are able to study the
Hindu hymns and prayers with intelligence
and insight, we cannot help declaring with
the Vedic seers : " The Being is one, but
sages call Him variously "—an idea expressed
so clearly and sincerely in the famous pas-
sage in the Mahimna Stotra : " Different are
the paths laid down in the Vedas, Sankhya,

Yoga, Shaiva and Vaishnava scriptures.
Of these, some people take to one and some
to another as the best. Devotees follow
these diverse paths, straight or crooked,
according to their different tendencies. Yet,
O Lord, Thou alone art the ultimate goal of
all men, as is the ocean of all rivers " (Universal Prayers, No. 214).

PLEA FOR RELIGIOUS TOLERATION AND
HARMONY

But it is not given to all to realise this
great ideal of synthesis and acceptance.
Devotees with a strongly sectarian bias very
often hold that salvation lies only through
the worship of their particular Deity or Incarnation, or through devotion to their formless or personal God who delivers His
message to mankind only through certain
prophets or teachers. But side by side with
men of circumscribed vision there are liberal
souls who, while they yield to none in their

love and faith for their chosen ideal, look upon all divine Personalities as manifestations of the same Truth : " I make no difference in substance between Shiva, the supreme Lord of the universe, and Vishnu, its inmost Self. But still may my devotion continue to be directed to Shiva " (Universal Prayers, No. 302).

A comparatively modern verse goes farther and speaks of this underlying harmony in the clearest terms : " Whether the highest Being is called Vishnu or Shiva, Brahmā or Indra, Sun or Moon, Buddha or the perfect Mahavir, I always offer my salutations to Him alone who is free from attachment and hatred, from worldliness and ignorance, who is endowed with compassion towards all creatures, and is possessed of all noble attributes " (Universal Prayers, No. 305).

Thus the conception of the unity behind the diversity has been a fundamental fact in the Hindu religious consciousness all along its unbroken course—an idea that was very

positively proclaimed by Manu : " One ought
to know the supreme Spirit who is the ruler
of all, subtler than the subtlest, of resplendent glory, and capable of being realised only
by meditation. Some call Him Agni (the
adorable) ; others call Him Manu (the
thinker) ; and others Prajapati (the lord of
creatures). Some again call Him Indra (the
glorious), others Prana (the source of life),
and still others the eternal Brahman (the
great) " (Manu, XII, 122, 123).

Persons who cannot rise above the idea of
multiplicity and limitations understand by
the terms Agni etc., only the different
gods. But those who can take a higher
view, mean by them the different aspects
or attributes of the same divine Being.
Truly speaking, there have been monotheistic and monistic interpreters who have
always considered the various names to
be different attributes of one and the same
God. And in this respect the commenta-
tor of the Vishnu Sahasranama has little

difference with the monotheistic interpreters of the modern Arya Samaj.

Indeed, the Personal, conceived under whatever name or form—be it as a God or as an Incarnation—if It be regarded as an expression of the Impersonal, then in the common worship of this personal-impersonal or the impersonal-personal Being, the followers of all religions and creeds may join their hands and hearts. And special stress should be laid in modern times on the recognition of this universal aspect of the divine Being, so that it may serve as the great bond for uniting the truly pious in all religions and countries, and for making them work together for the commonweal in a spirit of brotherhood and fellowship, service and co-operation.

" May He, the One without a second, who, though formless, produces by means of His manifold powers, various forms without any purpose of His own ; from whom the universe comes into being in the beginning of creation, and to whom it returns in the end, endow us with good thoughts " (Universal Prayers, No. 42).

And—" May He, the indwelling Spirit, the remover of all sins, the presiding Deity of all undertakings, be pleased. For, He being pleased, the whole universe is pleased ; He being satisfied, the whole universe is satisfied " (Universal Prayers, No. 316).

Madras,
November, 1933   SWAMI YATISWARANANDA

समानो मन्त्रस्समितिस्समानी ।
समानं मनस्सह चित्तमेषाम् ॥

समानी व आकूतिस्समाना हृदयानि वः ।
समानमस्तु वो मनो यथा वस्सुसहासति ॥

Common be your prayer ;
Common be your end ;
Common be your purpose ;
Common be your deliberation.

Common be your desires ;
Unified be your hearts ;
United be your intentions ;
Perfect be the union amongst you.

Rig Veda, X, 191-3, 4.

ॐ असतो मा सद्गमय ।

तमसो मा ज्योतिर्गमय ।

मृत्योर्मामृतं गमय ॥

ॐ पूर्णमदः पूर्णमिदं पूर्णात्पूर्णमुदच्यते ।

पूर्णस्य पूर्णमादाय पूर्णमेवावशिष्यते ॥

ॐ शान्तिः । शान्तिः । शान्तिः ॥

Om. *From the unreal lead me to the Real.*
     From darkness lead me to Light.
     From death lead me to Immortality.
          Brihadaranyakopanishad, I, 3, 28.

Om. *All that is invisible is verily the Infi-*
     nite Brahman. All that is visible is
     also the Infinite Brahman. The whole
     universe has come out of the Infinite
     Brahman. Brahman is infinite al-
     though the whole universe has come
     out of It.

          Om Peace, Peace, Peace.

          Brihadaranyakopanishad, V, 1, 1.

UNIVERSAL PRAYERS

FROM THE VEDAS

ओं भद्रं कर्णेभिः शृणुयाम देवाः
भद्रं पश्येमाक्षभिर्यजत्राः ।
स्थिरैरङ्गैस्तुष्टुवाꣳसस्तनूभिर्
व्यशेम देवहितं यदायुः ॥ १ ॥

ओं शान्तिः शान्तिः शान्तिः ॥

ओं वाङ् मे मनसि प्रतिष्ठिता मनो मे वाचि
प्रतिष्ठितम् । आविरावीर्म एधि । वेदस्य म
आणीम्थः श्रुतं मे मा प्रहासीः अनेनाधीतेनाहो-
रात्रान्सन्दधामि । ऋतं वदिष्यामि । सत्यं वदिष्यामि ।
तन्मामवतु । तद् वक्तारमवतु । अवतु माम् । अवतु
वक्तारमवतु वक्तारम् ॥ २ ॥

ओं शान्तिः शान्तिः शान्तिः ॥

1. Om. O Gods, may we hear with our ears what is auspicious. O Ye adorable ones, may we see with our eyes what is auspicious. May we sing praises to ye and enjoy with strong limbs and body the life allotted to us by the Gods.

Om Peace, Peace, Peace.

2. Om. May my speech be fixed in the mind. May my mind be fixed in the speech. O self-manifested Atman, do Thou manifest Thyself unto me. O my mind and speech, may ye be fit to reveal unto me the highest knowledge. May I not forget what I have heard. Without forgetting what I have learnt, may I be able to study day and night. The right will I speak. The truth will I speak. May Brahman protect me. May Brahman protect the preceptor. May Brahman protect me. May Brahman protect the preceptor.

Om Peace, Peace, Peace.

ओं आप्यायन्तु ममाङ्गानि वाक् प्राणश्चक्षुः
श्रोत्रमथो बलमिन्द्रियाणि च सर्वाणि । सर्वे ब्रह्मौपनिषदं
माऽहं ब्रह्म निराकुर्यां मा मा ब्रह्म निराकरोदनिरा-
करणमस्त्वनिराकरणं मेऽस्तु । तदात्मनि निरते य
उपनिषत्सु धर्मास्ते मयि सन्तु ते मयि सन्तु ॥ ३ ॥

ओं शान्तिः शान्तिः शान्तिः ॥

ओं सह नाववतु सह नौ भुनक्तु । सह वीर्यं
करवावहै । तेजस्विनावधीतमस्तु मा विद्विषावहै ॥४॥

ओं शान्तिः शान्तिः शान्तिः ॥

3. Om. May my limbs, speech, breath, eye, ear, strength and all senses become perfected. Everything is the Brahman proclaimed in the Upanishads. May I never deny Brahman. May Brahman never reject me. May there be no denial at all May there be no denial at least from me. May I, who am devoted to the Atman, be endowed with all the virtues taught in the Upanishads.

Om Peace, Peace, Peace.

4. Om. May Brahman protect us both, the preceptor and the disciple. May He nourish us both. May we work together with great energy. May our study be vigorous and fruitful. May we not hate each other.

Om Peace, Peace, Peace.

4

ओं द्यौः शान्तिरन्तरिक्षं शान्तिः पृथिवी शान्ति
रापः शान्तिरोषधयः शान्तिः । वनस्पतयः शान्ति-
र्विश्वेदेवाः शान्तिर्ब्रह्म शान्तिः सर्वं शान्तिः शान्ति-
रेव शान्तिः ॥ ५ ॥

ओं शं नो मित्रः शं वरुणः । शं नो भवत्वर्यमा ।
शं न इन्द्रो बृहस्पतिः । शं नो विष्णुरुरुक्रमः ।
नमो ब्रह्मणे । नमस्ते वायो । त्वमेव प्रत्यक्षं ब्रह्मासि ।
त्वामेव प्रत्यक्षं ब्रह्म वदिष्यामि । ऋतं वदिष्यामि ।
सत्यं वदिष्यामि । तन्मामवतु । तद्वक्तारमवतु ।
अवतु माम् । अवतु वक्तारम् ॥ ६ ॥
                ओं शान्तिः शान्तिः शान्तिः ॥

5. Om. May there be peace in heaven. May there be peace in the sky. May there be peace on earth. May there be peace in the water. May there be peace in the plants. May there be peace in the trees. May there be peace in the Gods. May there be peace in Brahman. May there be peace in all. May that peace, real peace, be mine.

6. Om. May the presiding deity of day be propitious to us. May the presiding deity of night be propitious to us. May the presiding deity of the sense of vision be propitious to us. May the Gods of strength and of intellect also be propitious to us. May the all-pervading Lord be propitious. Adoration to Brahman. Adoration to Thee, the controller of activities. Thou art, verily, the visible Brahman. Verily, I will declare Thee to be the visible Brahman. The right will I speak. The truth will I speak. May Brahman protect me. May Brahman protect the preceptor. May He protect me. May He protect the preceptor.

Om Peace, Peace, Peace.

हिरण्यगर्भः समवर्तताग्रे

भूतस्य जातः पतिरेक आसीत् ।

स दाधार पृथिवीं द्यामुतेमां

कस्मै देवाय हविषा विधेम ॥ ७ ॥

य आत्मदा बलदा यस्य विश्व

उपासते प्रशिषं यस्य देवाः ।

यस्य छायामृतं यस्य मृत्युः

कस्मै देवाय हविषा विधेम ॥ ८ ॥

यः प्राणतो निमिषतो महित्वैक

इद्राजा जगतो बभूव ।

य ईशे अस्य द्विपदश्चतुष्पदः

कस्मै देवाय हविषा विधेम ॥ ९ ॥

येन द्यौरुग्रा पृथिवी च दृढळा

येन स्वः स्तभितं येन नाकः ।

यो अन्तरिक्षे रजसो विमानः

कस्मै देवाय हविषा विधेम ॥ १० ॥

Rig Veda, X, 121, 1, 2, 3. 5.

7. In the beginning there existed God, the source of light. He was the one Lord of all created beings. He upholds this earth and the heavens. He it is to whom we offer our prayers.

8. He who is the giver of spiritual knowledge and strength, whom the world worships, whose command all learned men obey, whose shelter is immortality, whose shadow is death,—He it is to whom we offer our prayers.

9. He, whose greatness has made Him the one sole king of this animate and inanimate world, who is the creator and lord of all bipeds and quadrupeds,—He it is to whom we offer our prayers.

10. He, by whom the heavenly bodies are uplifted and the earth is made stable, by whom the firmament and heaven are established, who pervades the entire space by His spiritual essence,—He it is to whom we offer our prayers.

उप त्वाग्ने दिवे दिवे दोषावस्तर्धिया वयम् ।
नमो भरन्त एमसि ॥ ११ ॥

Rig Veda, I, 1, 7.

स नः पितेव सूनवेऽग्ने सूपायनो भव ।
सचस्वा नः स्वस्तये ॥ १२ ॥

Rig Veda, I, 1, 9.

यो विश्वाभि विपश्यति भुवना सं च पश्यति ।
स नः पूषाविता भुवत् ॥ १३ ॥

Rig Veda, III, 62, 9.

तत् सवितुर्वरेण्यं भर्गो देवस्य धीमहि ।
धियो यो नः प्रचोदयात् ॥ १४ ॥

Rig Veda, III, 62, 10.

अग्ने व्रतपते व्रतं चरिष्यामि तच्छकेयं तन्मे
राध्यताम् । इदमहमनृतात्सत्यमुपैमि ॥ १५ ॥

Sukla Yajur Veda Samhita, I, 5.

11. To Thee, O dispeller of gloom, we offer salutations with our mind, and approach Thee daily, by day and by night.

12. Be of easy approach to us, even as a father to his son. Do Thou, O self-effulgent Lord, abide with us and bring blessings to us.

13. The Lord who watches over the universe and fully understands the truth behind all things,—may He protect us all.

14. Let us meditate on the excellent glory of that divine Being who illumines everything. May He guide our understanding.

15. O Thou glorious Lord, O protector of vows, I am determined to master my lower self. Vouchsafe unto me the required strength and make my effort fruitful. Through Thy grace, leaving untruth, may I realise Truth.

ञ्यम्बकं यजामहे सुगन्धि पुष्टिवर्धनम् ।
उर्वारुकमिव बन्धनान्मृत्योर्मुक्षीय मामृतात् ॥ १६ ॥

> Sukla Yajur Veda Samhita, III, 60.

या ते रुद्र शिवा तनूरघोरापापकाशिनी ।
तया नस्तन्वा शन्तमया गिरिशन्त
    अभिचाकशीहि ॥ १७ ॥

> Sukla Yajur Veda Samhita, XVI, 2.

नमो भवस्य हेत्यै जगतां पतये नमः ॥ १८ ॥

> Sukla Yajur Veda Samhita, XVI, 18.

नमो भुवन्तये वारिवस्कृतायौषधीनां पतये नमः ॥१९॥

> Sukla Yajur Veda Samhita, XVI, 19.

16. I worship Thee, O sweet Lord of transcendental vision. O giver of prosperity to all, may I be free from the bonds of death, like a ripe fruit dropping from the tree. May I never again forget my immortal nature.

17. O Lord, Thou who blesseth all creatures by revealing the highest knowledge, deign to make us happy by Thy calm and blissful Self that roots out terror as well as sin.

18. Salutations to Thee, O destroyer of the cycle of births and deaths. Salutations to Thee, O Lord, of the universe.

19. Thou art, O Lord, the creator of the worlds. Salutations to Thee. Thou producest the herbs and plants as well. O Thou bestower of earthly felicity, salutations to Thee.

नम: शम्भवाय च मयोभवाय च ।

नम: शङ्कराय च मयस्कराय च ।

नम: शिवाय च शिवतराय च ॥ २० ॥

Sukla Yajur Veda Samhita, XVI, 41.

नम: पार्याय चावार्याय च ।

नम: प्रतरणाय चोत्तरणाय च ॥

नमस्तीर्थ्याय च कूल्याय च ।

नम: शष्प्याय च फेन्याय च ॥ २१ ॥

Sukla Yajur Veda Samhita, XVI, 42.

नम: सिकत्याय च प्रवाह्याय च ।

नम: किंशिलाय च क्षयणाय च ॥

नम: कपर्दिने च पुलस्तये च ।

नम: इरिण्याय च प्रपथ्याय च ॥ २२ ॥

Sukla Yajur Veda Samhita, XVI, 43.

20. We offer our salutations to Thee, the giver of happiness and well-being. We offer our salutations to Thee, the promoter of good and auspiciousness. We offer our salutations to Thee, the bestower of bliss and still greater bliss.

21. O Lord, Thou art beyond the sea of relative existence. Thou art also in the midst of it; I bow to Thee. Thou enablest one to go beyond sin by means of holy chants. Thou takest one beyond the cycle of births and deaths through knowledge; I bow to Thee. Thou art present in sacred flowing streams as well as on the coast; I bow to Thee. Thou art in the tender grass, on the sea-shore as well as in the foaming waves; I bow to Thee.

22. O Lord, thou art on the sand banks as well as in the midst of the current; I bow to Thee. Thou art in the little pebbles as well as in the calm expanse of the sea; I bow to Thee. O all-pervading Lord, Thou art in the barren soil and in crowded places; I bow to Thee.

या ते रुद्र शिवा तनू: शिवा विश्वाहा भेषजी ।

शिवा रुद्रस्य भेषजी तया नो मृड जीवसे ॥ २३ ॥

Sukla Yajur Veda Samhita, XVI, 49.

तेजोऽसि तेजो मयि धेहि । वीर्यमसि वीर्यं मयि
धेहि ।

बलमसि बलं मयि धेहि । ओजोऽसि ओजो मयि
धेहि ।

मन्युरसि मन्युं मयि धेहि । सहोऽसि सहो मयि
धेहि ॥ २४ ॥

Sukla Yajur Veda Samhita, XIX, 9.

विश्वानि देव सवितर्दुरितानि परासुव ।

यद्भद्रं तन्न आसुव ॥ २५ ॥

Sukla Yajur Veda Samhita, XXX, 3.

मित्रस्याहं चक्षुषा सर्वाणि भूतानि समीक्षे ।

मित्रस्य चक्षुषा समीक्षामहे ॥ २६ ॥

Sukla Yajur Veda Samhita, XXXVI, 18.

23. O Lord, Thy blissful Self removes all ills and roots out all pain. Do Thou make our lives happy and fruitful.

24. O Lord, Thou art the embodiment of infinite energy; do Thou fill me with energy. Thou art the embodiment of infinite virility; do Thou endow me with virility. Thou art the embodiment of infinite strength; do Thou bestow strength upon me. Thou art the embodiment of infinite power; do Thou grant power unto me. Thou art the embodiment of infinite courage; do Thou inspire me with courage. Thou art the embodiment of infinite fortitude; do Thou steel me with fortitude.

25. O Lord, O Thou the illuminator, do Thou free us from sins. Do Thou bring to us what is auspicious.

26. May I be able to look upon all beings with the eye of a friend. May we look upon one another with the eye of a friend.

पिता नोऽसि पिता नो बोधि ।
नमस्तेऽस्तु मा मा हिंसी: ॥ २७ ॥

Sukla Yajur Veda Samhita, XXXVII, 20.

तत् पुरुषाय विद्महे महादेवाय धीमहि
तन्नो रुद्र: प्रचोदयात् ॥ २८ ॥

Taittiriya Aranyaka, X, 1, 24.

वेदात्मनाय विद्महे हिरण्यगर्भाय धीमहि
तन्नो ब्रह्म प्रचोदयात् ॥ २९ ॥

Taittiriya Aranyka, X, 1, 29.

नारायणाय विद्महे वासुदेवाय धीमहि
तन्नो विष्णु: प्रचोदयात् ॥ ३० ॥

Taittiriya Aranyaka, X, 1, 30.

यन्मे मनसा वाचा कर्मणा वा दुष्कृतं कृतम् ।
तन्न इन्द्रो वरुणो बृहस्पति: सविता च पुनन्तु पुन:
पुन: ॥ ३१ ॥

Taittiriya Aranyaka, X, 1, 48.

27. O Lord, Thou art our father; do Thou instruct us like a father. We offer our salutations to Thee. Do Thou not destroy us; do Thou protect us ever.

28. We contemplate on the Indweller of all. We mediate upon the Lord supreme. May that destroyer of all ills ever direct us.

29. We contemplate on the embodiment of the highest wisdom. We meditate upon the very First Cause. May that Brahman— the infinite Being—ever guide our understanding.

30. We contemplate on the supreme abode of all. We meditate upon the effulgent yet unmanifest Being. May that all-pervading Lord ever inspire us.

31. Whatever sins have been committed by me, by thought, word or deed, may the supreme Lord, the source of strength, wisdom and purity, forgive me and cleanse me of them all.

सोऽहमपापो विरजो निर्मुक्तो मुक्तकिल्बिषः ।
नाकस्य पृष्ठमारुह्य गच्छेद्ब्रह्मसलोकताम् ॥ ३२ ॥

Taittiriya Aranyaka, X, 1, 52.

चरणं पवित्रं विततं पुराणं
  येन पूतस्तरति दुष्कृतानि ।
तेन पवित्रेण शुद्धेन पूताः
  अतिपाप्मानमरातिं तरेम ॥ ३३ ॥

Taittiriya Aranyaka, X, 11.

ब्रह्ममेतु माम् । मधुमेतु माम् ।
  ब्रह्ममेवमधुमेतु माम् ॥ ३४ ॥

Taittiriya Aranyaka, X, 38.

ब्रह्म मेधया । मधु मेधया । ब्रह्मेव मधुमेधया ॥ ३५ ॥

Taittiriya Aranyaka, X, 39.

32. Being free from sins and impurities, bondages and evils, may I soar up to the highest heavens; may I attain to the same abode as the almighty Brahman.

33. Being purified by the holy, all-pervading, eternal presence of the effulgent Being, man gets rid of evil. May we, too, go beyond the touch of sin, our great enemy, being freed from Impurity by that ever-holy Presence that purifies all.

34. May Brahman be realised by us. May the highest bliss be realised by us. May Brahman, who is the highest bliss, be realised by us.

35. May we realise Brahman with our purified understanding. May we realize the highest bliss with our purified understanding. May we realise Brahman, who is the highest bliss, with our purified understanding.

5

मधु वाता ऋतायते । मधु क्षरन्ति सिन्धवः ।
माध्वीर्नः सन्त्वोषधीः । मधु नक्तमुतोषसि । मधु-
मत् पार्थिवं रजः । मधु द्यौरस्तु नः पिता । मधुमान्नो
वनस्पतिः । मधुमानस्तु सूर्यः । माध्वीर्गावो भवन्तु
नः ॥ ३६ ॥

Taittiriya Aranyaka, X, 39,

आत्मा मे शुध्यन्तां ज्योतिरहं विरजा विपाप्मा
भूयासम् । अन्तरात्मा मे शुध्यन्तां ज्योतिरहं विरजा
विपाप्मा भूयासम् । परमात्मा मे शुध्यन्तां ज्योतिरहं
विरजा विपाप्मा भूयासम् ॥ ३७ ॥

Taittiriya Aranyaka, X, 66.

नमो ब्रह्मणे नमो अस्त्वग्नये
नमः पृथिव्यै नम ओषधीभ्यः ।
नमो वाचे नमो वाचस्पतये
नमो विष्णवे बृहते करोमि ॥ ३८ ॥

Taittiriya Aranyaka, 1, 30

36. May the winds bring us happiness. May the rivers carry happiness to us. May the herbs give us happiness. May night and day yield us happiness. May the dust of the earth bring us happiness. May the heavens give us happiness. May the trees give us happiness. May the sun pour down happiness. May the cows yield us happiness.

37. May my body become pure. May I be free from impurity and sin. May I realise myself as the light divine. May my mind become pure. May I be free from impurity and sin. May I realise myself as the light divine. May my Self become pure. May I be free from impurity and sin. May I realise myself as the light divine.

38. Salutations to Brahman. Salutions to the God in the fire. Salutations to the God in the earth. Salutations to the God in the plants. Salutations to the God in speech. Salutations to the Lord of speech. I offer my salutations to the supreme Being, the all-pervading Spirit.

हिरण्मयेन पात्रेण सत्यस्यापिहितं मुखम् ।
तत् त्वं पूषन्नपावृणु सत्यधर्माय दृष्टये ॥ ३९ ॥

Isavasyopanishad, 1, 15.

यो देवोऽग्नौ योऽप्सु यो विश्वं भुवनमाविवेश ।
य ओषधीषु यो वनस्पतिषु तस्मै देवाय नमो नमः ॥

Svetasvataropanishad, II, 17.

यो देवानां प्रभवश्चोद्भवश्च विश्वाधिपो रुद्रो महर्षिः ।
हिरण्यगर्भं जनयामास पूर्वं स नो बुध्या शुभया
संयुनक्तु ॥ ४१ ॥

Svetasvataropanishad, III, 4.

य एकोऽवर्णो बहुधा शक्तियोगात्
वर्णाननेकान्निहितार्थो दधाति ।
निचैति चान्ते विश्वमादौ स देवः
स नो बुध्या शुभया संयुनक्तु ॥ ४२ ॥

Svetasvataropanishad, IV, 1.

39. Under a golden brilliance the face of Truth lies hidden. Do Thou, O Protector, withdraw this cover, that I, devoted to Truth alone, may realise it.

40. Salutations to the God who is in the fire, who is in the water, who has pervaded the whole universe, who is in the plants, and who is in the trees.

41. May He, the creator and supporter of the gods, the lord of all, the destroyer of evil, the great seer, He who brought the cosmic Soul into being, endow us with good thoughts.

42. May He, the One without a second, who, though formless, produces, by means of His manifold powers, various forms without any purpose of His own; from whom the universe comes into being in the beginning of creation; and to whom it returns in the end—endow us with good thoughts.

त्वं स्त्री त्वं पुमानसि

त्वं कुमार उत वा कुमारी ।

त्वं जीर्णो दण्डेन वञ्चसि

त्वं जातो भवसि विश्वतोमुखः ॥ ४३ ॥

Svetasvataropanishad, 1V, 3.

अजात इत्येवं कश्चिद्भीरुः प्रतिपद्यते ।

रुद्र यत्ते दक्षिणं मुखं तेन मां पाहि नित्यम् ॥ ४४ ॥

Svetasvataropanishad, VI, 21.

यस्तूर्णनाभ इव तन्तुभिः प्रधानजैः स्वभावतः ।

देव एकः स्वमावृणोति स नो दधातु ब्रह्माप्ययम् ॥

Svetasvataropanishad, VI, 10.

स तन्मयो ह्यमृत ईशसंस्थो

ज्ञः सर्वगो भुवनस्यास्य गोप्ता ।

य ईशे अस्य जगतो नित्यमेव

नान्यो हेतुर्विद्यत ईशनाय ॥ ४६ ॥

43. Thou art woman; Thou art man; Thou art youth; Thou art maiden; Thou art the old man tottering on his staff; Thou dost appear born in manifold forms.

44. As Thou art unborn, one afraid of birth and death like me seeks refuge in Thee. O Thou destroyer of evil, let Thy gracious presence ever protect me.

45. May the effulgent Being, the One without a second, who, like a spider, spontaneously covers Himself with threads made out of His own creative powers, grant us union with himself, the Brahman.

46-48. He is the Self of the universe, the immortal being, the lord. He is the all-knowing, all-pervading protector of the universe. He alone rules the world for ever, and none else. Desirous of emancipation I seek refuge in that effulgent Being, whose light reveals the knowledge of the Atman;

यो ब्रह्माणं विदधाति पूर्वे

   यो वै वेदांश्च प्रहिणोति तस्मै

तं ह देवमात्मबुद्धिप्रकाशं

   मुमुक्षुर्वै शरणमह प्रपद्ये ॥ ४७ ॥

निष्कलं निष्क्रियं शान्तं निरवद्यं निरञ्जनम् ।

अमृतस्य परं सेतुं दग्धेन्धनमिवानलम् ॥ ४८ ॥

Svetasvataropanishad, VI, 17, 18, 19.

विश्वेश्वर नमस्तुभ्यं विश्वात्मा विश्वकर्मकृत् ।

विश्वभुग्विश्वमायुस्त्वं विश्वक्रीडारतिप्रभुः ॥ ४९ ॥

Maitrayanyupanishad, IV, 14.

नमः शान्तात्मने तुभ्यं नमो गुह्यतमाय च ।

अचिन्त्यायाप्रमेयाय अनादिनिधनाय च ॥ ५० ॥

Maitrayanyupanishad, IV, 15.

who first creates the cosmic Soul and delivers to him the supreme knowledge; who is without parts, without actions, tranquil, without fault, without taint; who is the supreme bridge to immortality, and is self-effulgent like a blazing fire consuming its fuel.

49. Obeisance to Thee, O lord of the universe. Thou art the soul and the maker of the universe. Thou art the universal enjoyer. Thou again art the universal life. Thou verily art the author of this sport of the universe.

50. I bow to Thee, O Thou blissful Self. I bow to Thee, O secret of secrets. Thou art beyond all thought and limitation. Thou art without beginning and without end. I bow to Thee.

तुभ्यं मह्यमनन्ताय मह्यं तुभ्यं चिदात्मने ।
नमस्तुभ्यं परेशाय नमो मह्यं शिवाय च । ॥ ५१ ॥

Sannyasopanishad, 32.

गमागमस्थं गमनादिशून्यं
चिद्रूपदीपं तिमिरान्धनाशत् ।
पश्यामि तं सर्वजनान्तरस्थं
नमामि हंसं परमात्मरूपम् ॥ ५२ ॥

Yogasikhopanishad, VI, 20.

51. Salutations to Thee as well as to Me, the Infinite. Salutations to Me as well as to Thee, the intelligent Being. Salutations to Thee, the supreme Lord. Salutations to Me, the Self auspicious.

52. The divine Being who dwells in the moving and the non-moving, but is Himself immutable; who is the light of knowledge and the dispeller of blinding darkness,— Him, the dweller in the heart of all beings, I behold. Him, the supreme Self, I salute.

UNIVERSAL PRAYERS

FROM PURANAS Etc.

PART I

कार्पण्यदोषोपहतस्वभावः

पृच्छामि त्वां धर्मसम्मूढचेताः ।

यच्छ्रेयः स्यान्निश्चितं ब्रूहि तन्मे

शिष्यस्तेऽहं शाधि मां त्वां प्रपन्नम् ॥ ५३ ॥

Bhagavad Gita, II, 7.

त्वमक्षरं परमं वेदितव्यं

त्वमस्य विश्वस्य परं निधानम् ।

त्वमव्ययः शाश्वतधर्मगोप्ता

सनातनस्त्वं पुरुषो मतो मे ॥ ५४ ॥

Bhagavad Gita, XI, 18.

त्वमादिदेवः पुरुषः पुराण-

स्त्वमस्य विश्वस्य परं निधानम् ।

वेत्तासि वेद्यं च परं च धाम

त्वया ततं विश्वमनन्तरूप ॥ ५५ ॥

Bhagavad Gita, XI, 38.

53.   O Lord, with my nature overpowered by weak commiseration, with my mind thrown into confusion about duty, I supplicate Thee.   Tell me decidedly what is good for me.   I am Thy disciple.   Instruct me who have taken refuge in Thee.

54.   Thou art the imperishable, the supreme Being, the one to be known.   Thou art the great refuge of this universe.   Thou art the unchanging guardian of the eternal religion.   Thou art, I know, the most ancient being.

55.   O Thou of boundless forms ! Thou art the primal God of gods, the ancient being.   Thou art the supreme refuge of the universe.   Thou art the knower, and the one to be known.   Thou art the supreme goal.   By Thee is the universe pervaded.

वायुर्यमोऽग्निर्वरुणः शशाङ्कः

    प्रजापतिस्त्वं प्रपितामहश्च ।

नमो नमस्तेऽस्तु सहस्रकृत्वः

    पुनश्च भूयोऽपि नमो नमस्ते ॥ ५६ ॥

Bhagavad Gita, XI, 39.

नमः पुरस्तादथ पृष्ठतस्ते

    नमोऽस्तु ते सर्वत एव सर्वे ।

अनन्तवीर्यामितविक्रमस्त्वं

    सर्वं समाप्नोषि ततोऽसि सर्वः ॥ ५७ ॥

Bhagavad Gita, XI, 40.

पिताऽसि लोकस्य चराचरस्य

    त्वमस्य पूज्यश्च गुरुर्गरीयान् ।

न त्वत्समोऽस्त्यभ्यधिकः कुतोऽन्यो

    लोकत्रयेऽप्यप्रतिमप्रभाव ॥ ५८ ॥

Bhagavad Gita, XI, 43.

56. Thou art the god of wind, of death and of fire, the god of waters and of the moon. Thou art the creator, Thou art the creator of the creator. Salutations to Thee a thousand times, and again and again salutations to Thee.

57. Salutations to Thee before and to Thee behind. Salutations to Thee on every side. O Lord, Thou art everything. Infinite in power and infinite in prowess, Thou pervadest all. Therefore Thou art the all.

58. Thou art the father of the world, of the moving and the non-moving. Greater than the greatest, Thou art the one object of worship. There is none equal to Thee in all the worlds. Who, then, can excel Thee, O Thou of incomparable power?

6

तस्मात् प्रणम्य प्रणिधाय कायं
 प्रसादये त्वामहमीशमीड्यम्
पितेव पुत्रस्य सखेव सख्युः
 प्रिय: प्रियायार्हसि देव सोढुम् ॥ ५९ ॥

Bhagavad Gita, XI, 44.

ऊर्ध्वमूलमध:शाखमश्वत्थं प्राहुरव्ययम्
छन्दांसि यस्य पर्णानि यस्तं वेद स वेदवित् ॥ ६० ॥

अधश्चोर्ध्वं प्रसृतास्तस्य शाखा
 गुणप्रवृद्धा विषयप्रवाला: ।
अधश्च मूलान्यनुसन्ततानि
 कर्मानुबन्धीनि मनुष्यलोके ॥ ६१ ॥

न रूपमस्येह तथोपलभ्यते
 नान्तो न चादिर्न च सम्प्रतिष्ठा ।
अश्वत्थमेनं सुविरूढमूल-
 मसङ्गशस्त्रेण दृढेन छित्त्वा ॥ ६२ ॥

59.   Therefore, I prostrate myself before Thee in adoration, and crave Thy forgiveness. Forgive me, O Lord, as a father forgives his son, a friend his friend, a lover his beloved.

60.   They speak of an eternal Asvattha —the ever-changing tree of phenomenal existence—rooted above, and branching below. He who knows it is a man of knowledge.

61.   Its branches are spread below and above, nourished by the Gunas.   The sense-objects are its buds, and its roots stretch down below in the world of men, creating actions.

62-63.   Its form is not visible here— neither its end, nor origin, nor its basis. Having cut down this firm-rooted tree by the mighty sword of non-attachment,

ततः पदं तत् परिमार्गितव्यं
यस्मिन् गता न निवर्तन्ति भूयः ।
तमेव चाद्यं पुरुषं प्रपद्ये
यतः प्रवृत्तिः प्रसृता पुराणी ॥ ६३ ॥

Bhagavad Gita, XV, 1—4

महतस्तमसः पारे पुरुषं ह्यतितेजसम् ।
यं ज्ञात्वा मृत्युमत्येति तस्मै ज्ञेयात्मने नमः ॥ ६४ ॥

Mahabharata, Santiparva, XLVII, 40.

अपुण्यपुण्योपरमे यं पुनर्भवनिर्भयाः ।
शान्ताः सन्न्यासिनो यान्ति तस्मै मोक्षात्मने नमः ॥

Santiparva, XLVII, 55.

यस्मिन् सर्वे यतः सर्वे यः सर्वे सर्वतश्च यः ।
यश्च सर्वमयो देवस्तस्मै सर्वात्मने नमः ॥ ६६ ॥

Santiparva, XLVII, 83.

that goal is to be sought after, attaining which the wise do not return again. I take refuge in that primeval Being, from whom streams forth the eternal creative Energy.

64. The supremely effulgent Being, beyond the great darkness of ignorance, knowing whom one transcends death,— salutations to Him, the greatest object of knowledge.

65. Tranquil men of renunciation attain their salvation in Him, having their merits and demerits destroyed, and being freed from the fear of rebirth. Salutations to Him who exists in the form of salvation.

66. In Him all things exist; from Him they all originate. He has become all; He exists on every side. He is verily the All. Salutations to Him who is the soul of everything.

जितं ते पुण्डरीकाक्ष नमस्ते विश्वभावन ।
नमस्तेऽस्तु हृषीकेश महापुरुष पूर्वज ॥ ६७ ॥

Pancharatra, Jitamtestotra, I, 1.

एकस्त्वमसि लोकस्य स्रष्टा संहारकस्तथा ।
अध्यक्षश्चानुमन्ता च गुणमायासमावृतः ॥ ६८ ॥

Jitamtestotra, I, 3.

संसारसागरं घोरमनन्तक्लेशभाजनम् ।
त्वामेव शरणं प्राप्य निस्तरन्ति मनीषिणः ॥ ६९ ॥

Jitamtestotra, I, 4.

न ते रूपं न चाकारो नायुधानि न चास्पदम् ।
तथाऽपि पुरुषाकारो भक्तानां त्वं प्रकाशसे ॥ ७० ॥

Jitamtestotra, I, 5.

नैव किञ्चित् परोक्षं ते प्रत्यक्षोऽसि न कस्यचित् ।
नैव किञ्चिदसिद्धं ते न च सिद्धोऽसि कस्यचित् ॥

Jitamtestotra, I , 6

67. Glory unto Thee, O Lord of beauty. Salutations unto Thee, O creator of the universe. Thou art the ruler of the senses, the almighty being, the first-born. Salutations unto Thee.

68. O Lord, Thou art the sole creator, destroyer and presiding lord of the universe. Thou again art the eternal controller and guide. Thou art veiled by ignorance and differentiating attributes.

69. The wise, attaining to Thee alone the surest refuge, cross the terrible ocean of birth and death, the cause of endless pain and misery.

70. Thou hast no colour, no form, no weapons, no particular abode. Yet thou revealest Thyself unto Thy devotees in a personal form.

71. Nothing is beyond Thy ken, but Thou art not perceived by any. Nothing is unrealised by Thee, yet Thou art not realised by any.

कार्याणां कारणं पूर्वे वचसां वाच्यमुत्तमम् ।
योगानां परमां सिद्धिं परमं ते पदं विदुः ॥ ७२ ॥

Jitamtestotra, I, 7.

पाहि पाहि जगन्नाथ कृपया भक्तवत्सल ।
अनाथोऽहमधन्योऽहमकृतार्थः कथंचन ॥ ७३ ॥

Jitamtestotra, II, 10.

लोकानां त्वं परो धर्मः पुरुषः पुरुषोत्तमः ।
शरण्यं शरणं च त्वामाहुर्दिव्या महर्षयः ॥ ७४ ॥

Valmikiramayana, VI, cxix, 14, 15, 17.

दृश्यसे सर्वभूतेषु ब्राह्मणेषु च गोषु च ।
दिक्षु सर्वासु गगने पर्वतेषु नदीषु च ॥ ७५ ॥

Valmikiramayana, VI, cxix, 20, 21.

72. The sages know Thee to be the primary cause of things, the greatest of the objects ever expressed in words, and the ultimate goal of all spiritual paths. Thou art verily the supreme existence.

73. Lord of the universe, lover of Thy devotees, with Thy grace, do Thou somehow save me who am helpless, unhappy and disappointed through my failure to attain the goal.

74. O Lord, Thou art the embodiment of the highest virtue in all the worlds. Thou art the indweller, the supreme Being. Holy sages proclaim Thee as the greatest refuge and saviour of mankind.

75. Thou art manifest in all creatures, in the animal as well as in the holy man. Thou art manifest in all directions, in the sky as well as in rivers and mountains.

सहस्रचरणः श्रीमान् शतशीर्षः सहस्रदृक् ।
त्वं धारयसि भूतानि पृथिवीं सर्वपर्वतान् ॥ ७६ ॥

Valmikiramayana, VI, cxix, 21, 22.

जगतामादिभूतस्त्वं जगत् त्वं जगदाश्रयः ।
सर्वभूतेष्वसंयुक्त एको भाति भवान् परः ॥ ७७ ॥

Adhyatmaramayana, I, v, 52.

आकाशवत् त्वं सर्वत्र बहिरन्तर्गतोऽमलः ।
असङ्गो ह्यचलो नित्यः शुद्धो बुद्धः सदव्ययः ॥७८॥

Adhyatmaramayana, I, v, 56.

देव मे यत्रकुत्रापि स्थितायाः अपि सर्वदा ।
त्वत्पादकमले सक्ता भक्तिरेव सदास्तु मे ॥ ७९ ॥

Adhyatmaramayana, I, v, 58.

नमस्ते पुरुषाध्यक्ष नमस्ते भक्तवत्सल ।
नमस्तेऽस्तु हृषीकेश नारायण नमोऽस्तु ते ॥ ८० ॥

Adhyatmaramayana, I, v, 59.

76. Thou art the most glorious cosmic Being with innumerable feet, hands and eyes. Thou art the supporter of the world of beings and of the earth with the mountains.

77. Thou art, O supreme Lord, the cause, the manifestation as also the support of this universe; yet Thou shinest as the one absolute existence unaffected by the changes in things.

78. Stainless, Thou pervadest this universe both inside and outside, like the sky. Thou art the uncontaminated, changeless and indestructible, the pure and eternal wisdom and truth.

79. Wherever I be, O Lord, may I always have unflinching devotion to Thy lotus feet.

80. Salutations unto Thee, O lord of all beings and lover of devotees. Salutations unto Thee, O Lord all-pervading, who art the master of the senses.

त्वं शुद्धबोधोऽसि हि सर्वदेहिना
मात्मास्यधीशोऽसि निराकृतिः स्वयम् ।
प्रतीयसे ज्ञानदृशां महामते
पादाब्जभृङ्गाहितसङ्गसङ्गिनाम् ॥ ८१ ॥

Adhyatmaramayana, VII, v, 4.

अहं प्रपन्नोऽस्मि पदाम्बुजं प्रभो
भवापवर्गे तव योगिभावितम् ।
यथाञ्जसाज्ञानमपारवारिधिं
सुखं तरिष्यामि तथानुशाधि माम् ॥ ८२ ॥

Adhyatmaramayana, VII, v, 5.

योऽन्तः प्रविश्य मम वाचमिमां प्रसुप्तां
सञ्जीवयत्यखिलशक्तिधरः स्वधाम्ना ।
अन्यांश्च हस्तचरणश्रवणत्वगादीन्
प्राणान् नमो भगवते पुरुषाय तुभ्यम् ॥ ८३ ॥

Bhagavata, IV, 9, 6.

81. O Lord omniscient, Thou verily art the absolute Consciousness, the Atman and master of all beings, the formless Reality. Thou revealest Thyself unto those whose eye of knowledge has opened, and who, like the bee, have their mind ever fixed on Thy lotus feet.

82. O Lord, I seek the shelter of Thy lotus feet which Yogins ever meditate upon and which verily sever all shackles that bind man to earth. Do Thou show unto me the way by which I may truly cross this shoreless ocean of ignorance with ease.

83. O Lord, I make salutations to Thee, the glorious Being. Thou hast entered into me through Thy intelligent power and roused my dormant faculty of speech. Being the lord of all powers, Thou kindlest to activity also all other organs of mine.

स्वस्यस्तु विश्वस्य खलः प्रसीदतां
    ध्यायन्तु भूतानि शिवं मिथो धिया ।
मनश्च भद्रं भजतादधोक्षज
    आवेश्यतां नो मतिरप्यहैतुकी ॥ ८४ ॥

Bhagavata, V, 18, 9.

मन्ये धनाभिजनरूपतपः श्रुतौज-
    स्तेजः प्रभावबलपौरुषबुद्धियोगाः ।
नाराधनाय हि भवन्ति परस्य पुंसो
    भक्त्या तुतोष भगवान् गजयूथपाय ॥ ८५ ॥

Bhagavata, VII, 9, 9.

विप्राद्द्विषड्गुणयुतादरविन्दनाभ-
    पादारविन्दविमुखाच्छ्वपचं वरिष्ठम् ।
मन्ये तदर्पितमनोवचनेहितार्थे-
    प्राणं पुनाति स कुलं न तु भूरिमानः ॥ ८६ ॥

Bhagavata, VII, 9, 10.

84. May the world be peaceful. May the wicked become gentle. May all creatures think of mutual welfare. May their minds be occupied with what is auspicious. And may our hearts be immersed in selfless love for the Lord.

85. Wealth, noble ancestry, physical beauty, asceticism, scriptural knowledge, power, energy, courage, might, diligence, prudence and Yogic practice—all these I deem of no avail in the worship of the supreme Being. For, indeed, the almighty Lord is pleased with the devotee not for anything else but for his great devotion to Him.

86. I consider even the lowest-born man, who has dedicated his thoughts, words, efforts, riches and life to the Lord, to be worthier than the Brahmin—the highest-born—who, though possessing the above-mentioned twelve qualities, is disinclined to worship the lotus feet of the Lord; for the former sanctifies his race, but not so the latter who is puffed up with immense conceit.

त्रस्तोऽस्म्यहं कृपणवत्सल दुस्सहोग्र-

संसारचक्रकदनाद् ग्रसतां प्रणीतः ।

बद्धः स्वकर्मभिरुशत्तम तेऽङ्घ्रिमूलं

प्रीतोऽपवर्गशरणं ह्वयसे कदा नु ॥ ८७ ॥

Bhagavata, VII, 9, 16,

नैवोद्विजे परदुरत्ययवैतरिण्या-

त्वद्वीर्यगायनमहाऽमृतमग्नचित्तः ।

शोचे ततो विमुखचेतस इन्द्रियार्थ-

मायासुखाय भरमुद्वहतो विमूढान् ॥ ८८ ॥

Bhagavata, VII, 9, 43.

नमो भगवते तस्मै यत एतच्चिदात्मकम् ।

पुरुषायादिबीजाय परेशायाभिधीमहि ॥ ८९ ॥

Bhagavata, VIII, 3, 2.

87. O Lord who art kind to the help-less, terribly afraid am I of the unbearable and dreadful woe that overtakes those who turn round and round in the wheel of exis-tence. Bound though I be by the conse-quences of my actions, O most glorious one, when shalt Thou, being propitious, recall me unto Thy blessed feet that bestow salva-tion and protection ?

88. With my mind absorbed in the bliss of singing Thy glory, O supreme Lord, I fear not the dreadful river of existence, difficult to cross ; but I feel sorry for the pitiable condition of those perverted souls who labour under the dead weight of the world, tempted by the illusions of sensual enjoyments.

89. We offer our salutations to the Lord who endows all beings with consciousness. We meditate on Him, the great Being, who is the origin of the universe and is the supreme Lord.

यस्मिन्निदं यतश्चेदं येनेदं य इदं स्वयम् ।
योऽस्मात् परस्माच्च परस्तं प्रपद्ये स्वयम्भुवम् ॥ ९० ॥

Bhagavata, VIII, 3, 3.

तस्मै नमः परेशाय ब्रह्मणेऽनन्तशक्तये ।
अरूपायोरुरूपाय नम आश्चर्यकर्मणे ॥ ९१ ॥

Bhagavata, VIII, 3, 9.

नम आत्मप्रदीपाय साक्षिणे परमात्मने ।
नमो गिरां विदूराय मनश्चेतसामपि ॥ ९२ ॥

Bhagavata, VIII, 3, 10.

नमः शान्ताय घोराय गूढाय गुणधर्मिणे ।
निर्विशेषाय साम्याय नमो ज्ञानघनाय च ॥ ९३ ॥

Bhagavata, VIII, 3, 12

90. I take refuge in the self-existent Being in whom the universe rests, from whom it has sprung, by whom it has been brought into being, who Himself constitutes it, and who is at the same time destinct from both cause and effect.

91. Salutations unto the highest Lord, unto Brahman, unto Him of infinite power, who is without any form and yet is the possessor of countless forms, who is the doer of wonderful deeds.

92. Salutations unto the Lord who is the light of the soul, the witness and the spirit supreme. Salutations unto Him who is beyond speech, nay, even beyond thought and beyond consciousness.

93. Salutations unto Him who is peaceful yet terrific, who has no attributes but who acts as the support of all attributes, who is Himself without difference, who is ever the same, and who is knowledge personified

क्षेत्रज्ञाय नमस्तुभ्यं सर्वाध्यक्षाय साक्षिणे ।
पुरुषायात्ममूलाय मूलप्रकृतये नमः ॥ ९४ ॥

Bhagavata, VIII, 3, 13.

नमो नमस्तेऽखिलकारणाय
    निष्कारणायाद्भुतकारणाय ।
सर्वागमाम्नाय महार्णवाय
    नमोऽपवर्गाय परायणाय ॥ ९५ ॥

Bhagavata, VIII, 3, 15.

सत्यव्रतं सत्यपरं त्रिसत्यं
    सत्यस्य योनिं निहितं च सत्ये ।
सत्यस्य सत्यमृतसत्यनेत्रं
    सत्यात्मकं त्वां शरणं प्रपन्नाः ॥ ९६ ॥

Bhagavata, X, 2, 26.

94.   Salutations, O Lord, unto Thee, the Self, the sovereign and the witness of all. Salutations unto Thee, the great Being, the origin of souls, and the source even of the primal matrix of creation.

95.   Salutations unto Thee, O Lord. Thou art the cause of all, but art Thyself causeless.   Thou art the wonderful origin of the entire creation.   As the mighty ocean to rivers, Thou art the goal of all scriptures, the great refuge of all creatures and the bestower of emancipation.   Salutations unto Thee.

96.   O Lord, Thou art of infallible will, and art attainable through truthfulness alone. Thou art Truth in the past, present and future.   Thou art the origin of the entire creation ; Thou dost pervade it, and art its true essence.   Thou dost direct truthful speech and conduct.   Thou art the embodiment of Truth.   In Thee do we take refuge.

कृष्ण कृष्ण महायोगिन् त्वमाद्यः पुरुषः परः ।
व्यक्ताव्यक्तमिदं विश्वं रूपं ते ब्राह्मणा विदुः ॥९७॥
त्वमेकः सर्वभूतानां देहास्वात्मेन्द्रियेश्वरः ।
त्वमेव कालो भगवान् विष्णुरव्यय ईश्वरः ॥ ९८ ॥

Bhagavata, X, 10, 29, 30.

वाणी गुणानुकथने श्रवणौ कथायाम्
हस्तौ च कर्मसु मनस्तव पादयोर्नः ।
स्मृत्यां शिरस्तव निवासजगत्प्रणामे
दृष्टिः सतां दर्शनेऽस्तु भवत्तनूनाम् ॥ ९९ ॥

Bhagavata, X, 10, 38.

एकस्त्वमात्मा पुरुषः पुराणः
सत्यः स्वयञ्ज्योतिरनन्त आद्यः ।
नित्योऽक्षरोऽजस्रसुखो निरञ्जनः
पूर्णोऽद्वयो मुक्त उपाधितोऽमृतः ॥ १०० ॥

Bhagavata, X, 14, 23.

97-98.   O charming Lord, Yogin supreme,
Thou art the perfect and primal Being. The
universe, both manifest and unmanifest, the
wise know as Thy body. Thou art the sole
master of body, life, mind and senses of all
beings. Thou, verily, art Time. Thou art
the all-pervading Being, the possessor of all
glories, the Lord omnipotent and changeless.

99.   Let our speech be devoted to the
narration of Thy excellence, our ears to the
hearing of Thy wonderful glory, our hands
to the performance of Thy work, our minds
to meditation on Thy holy feet, our heads to
bowing to the world—Thy abode—and our
eyes to seeing the righteous who are Thy
body.

100.   O Lord, Thou art the One, the
Self, the indwelling Spirit, the ancient one.
Thou art the Truth, self-effulgent, infinite
and primal. Thou art eternal, imperishable,
and of the nature of bliss everlasting, and
untainted. Thou art perfect, without a
second, absolute and immortal.

यं ब्रह्मा वरुणेन्द्ररुद्रमरुतः स्तुन्वन्ति दिव्यैस्तवै-
   र्वेदैः साङ्गपदक्रमोपनिषदैर्गायन्ति यं सामगाः ।
ध्यानावस्थिततद्गतेन मनसा पश्यन्ति यं योगिनो
   यस्यान्तं न विदुः सुरासुरगणा देवाय तस्मै नमः ॥

Bhagavata, XII, 13, 1.

सर्वस्मिन् सर्वभूतस्त्वं सर्वः सर्वस्वरूपधृक् ।
सर्वे त्वत्तस्ततश्च त्वं नमः सर्वात्मनेऽस्तुते ॥ १०२ ॥

Vishnupurana, I, 12, 71.

सर्वात्मकोऽसि सर्वेश सर्वभूतस्थितो यतः ।
कथयामि ततः किं ते सर्वं वेत्सि हृदिस्थितम् ॥१०३॥

Vishnupurana, I, 12, 72.

सर्वात्मन् सर्वभूतेश सर्वसत्त्वसमुद्भव ।
सर्वभूतो भवान् वेत्ति सर्वसत्त्वमनोरथम् ॥ १०४ ॥

Vishnupurana, I, 12, 73.

101. Salutations to that effulgent Being whom Brahmā and other gods praise with divine hymns; whom the singers of the Sama glorify by the Vedas and their auxiliaries, repeating the words in a particular order along with the Upanishads; whom the Yogins realise through deep meditation with their minds wholly absorbed in Him; and whose extent neither the gods nor demons know.

102. Lord, Thou abidest in all; Thou art all; Thou assumest all forms; Thou art the origin of all. Thou art the Self of all. Salutations unto Thee.

103. Thou art the Self of all, O Lord of all and the indweller of all beings. What then shall I speak unto Thee who knowest my inmost thoughts?

104. O Thou, the Self of all beings, the sovereign lord of all creation, the source of all that exists. Thou who hast become all creatures knowest their desires.

नमस्तस्मै नमस्तस्मै नमस्तस्मै महात्मने ।
नामरूपं न यस्यैको योऽस्तित्वेनोपलभ्यते ॥ १०५ ॥

Vishnupurana, I, 19, 79.

योऽन्तस्तिष्ठन्नशेषस्य पश्यतीशः शुभाशुभम् ।
तं सर्वसाक्षिणं विष्णुं नमस्ये परमेश्वरम् ॥ १०६ ॥

Vishnupurana, I, 19, 81.

नमोऽस्तु विष्णवे तस्मै यस्याभिन्नमिदं जगत् ।
ध्येयः स जगतामाद्यः प्रसीदतु ममाव्ययः ॥ १०७ ॥

Vishnupurana, I, 19, 82.

न त्वहं कामये राज्यं न स्वर्गं नापुनर्भवम् ।
कामये दुःखतप्तानां प्राणिनामार्तिनाशनम् ॥ १०८ ॥

त्वं परं परमं तेजो मङ्गलानां च मङ्गलम् ।
अप्रमेयगुणश्चैव मन्त्राणां मन्त्रगो भवान् ॥ १०९ ॥

Skandapurana, I. ii. Ch. 29, Verse 126.

105. Salutations to the great Being beyond name and form, who is realised as the one existence. Salutations to Him, salutations to Him.

106. He dwells in all without exception, and is the witness of both good and bad. Salutations to Him, the all-pervading, the eternal witness, the Lord supreme.

107. Salutations to Him, the omnipresent, from whom the universe is inseparable. He, the first cause of the universe, is the one fit object of meditation. May He, the changless one, be propitious.

108. O Lord, I do not want any kingdom, nor heavenly pleasure, nor even escape from rebirth. But I do want that the affliction of all beings tormented by the miseries of life may cease.

109. Thou art the supreme Being, the supreme light, the most auspicious of the auspicious. Thou art the possessor of countless virtues, the secret import of the Mantras.

त्वं भर्ता सर्वभूतात्मा त्वं त्राता त्वं सुखावहः ।
त्वं कर्ता त्वं विधाता च चित्यो नित्यारिमर्दनः ॥११०॥

Skandapurana, I. ii. Ch. 29, Verses 131, 132.

कृतज्ञो वरदः सत्यः शरण्यः साधुवत्सलः ।
अपारपारो दुर्ज्ञेयः सर्वभूतहिते रतः ॥ १११ ॥

Skandapurana, I. ii. Ch. 29, Verses 135, 140.

अग्राह्यः कारणं कर्ता परमेष्ठी परं पदम् ।
अचिन्त्यः सर्वभूतात्मा सर्वात्मा त्वं सनातनः ॥११२॥

Skandapurana, I. ii. Ch. 29, Verses 140, 141.

नमस्तुभ्यं नमो मह्यं तुभ्यं मह्यं नमो नमः ।
अहं त्वं त्वमहं सर्वे जगदेतच्चराचरम् ॥ ११३ ॥

Skandapurana, II. ii. Ch. 27, Verse 15.

110. Thou art the supporter, the Self of all beings, the saviour, and the source of bliss. Thou art the master, the creator, the eternal Being, the eternal conqueror of enemies.

111. Thou takest note of the services of Thy devotees; and Thou also bestowest boons on them. Thou art the Truth eternal, the refuge, ever kind to the good. Thou art the deliverer from the limitless ocean of existence, the unknowable, the one devoted to the welfare of all beings.

112. Thou art the incomprehensible, the first cause, the creator, the supreme Deity and the supreme abode. Thou art the one beyond thought, the Self of all, the Self of the world, the eternal Being.

113. O Lord, salutations to Thee; salutations to Me; salutations to both Thee and Me. For, I am verily Thyself and Thou art Myself. Nay, Thou art the whole world, the moving and non-moving.

मदादिकमिदं सर्वे मायाविलसितं तव ।
अध्यस्तं त्वयि विश्वात्मन् त्वयैव परिणामितम् ॥११४॥

Skandapurana, II. ii. Ch. 27, Verse 16.

गुणातीत गुणाधार त्रिगुणात्मन्नमोऽस्तु ते ।
नमोऽचिन्त्यमहिम्ने ते चिद्रूपाय नमो नमः ॥ ११५ ॥

Skandapurana, II. ii. Ch. 27, Verses 21, 26.

नमो देवाधिदेवाय देवदेवाय ते नमः ।
दिव्यादिव्यस्वरूपाय दिव्यरूपाय ते नमः ॥ ११६ ॥

Skandapurana, II. ii. Ch. 27, Verses 26, 27.

जरामृत्युविहीनाय मृत्युरूपाय ते नमः ।
ज्वलदग्निस्वरूपाय मृत्योरपि च मृत्यवे ॥ ११७ ॥

Skandapurana, II. ii. Ch. 27, Verses 27, 28

114. Myself and everything else are creations of Thy divine power. O Thou soul of the world, everything is created by Thee and is superimposed on Thee.

115. Thou art beyond the Gunas,[1] the abode of the Gunas, the self of the Gunas; salutations to Thee. Thou art of glory unthinkable, and consciousness pure; salutations to Thee.

116. O Lord, Thou art the God of gods, the overlord; salutations unto Thee. Thou art of divine form, and withal both divine and non-divine.

117. Salutations unto Thee. Thou art death itself and withal beyond decay or death. Again, (being the destroyer of death), Thou art death unto death itself. Thou art bright and radiant like the burning fire. Salutations unto Thee.

---

[1] See Introduction to "Divine Life," pp. 21, etc.

प्रपन्नमृत्युनाशाय सहजानन्दरूपिणे ।
भक्तप्रियाय जगतां मात्रे पित्रे नमो नमः ॥ ११८ ॥

Skandapurana, II. ii. Ch. 27, Verse 28.

प्रपन्नार्तिविनाशाय नित्योद्योगिन् नमोऽस्तु ते ।
नमो नमस्ते दीनानां कृपासहजसिन्धवे ॥ ११९ ॥

Skandapurana, II. ii. Ch. 27, Verse 29.

एकं ब्रह्मैवाद्वितीयं समस्तं
    सत्यं सत्यं नेतरच्चास्ति किञ्चित् ।
एको रुद्रो न द्वितीयोऽवतस्थे
    तस्मादेकं त्वां प्रपद्ये महेशम् ॥ १२० ॥

Skandapurana, IV, Pt. I, Ch. X, Verse 126.

118. Thou art the ever-blissful Being, the destroyer of death to Thy servants. Thou lovest Thy devotees ; Thou art the father and mother of all. Salutations unto Thee.

Skandapurana, IV, Pt. I, Ch. X, 27.

119. Salutations to Thee who art ever interested in destroying the miseries of devotees. Thou art the infinite ocean of grace to the weak and lowly. Salutations unto Thee.

Skandapurana, IV, Pt. I, Ch. X, 128.

120. O Lord, Thou art the one Brahman without a second. Thou art everything. Thou art the one Truth, and verily there is nothing but Thee. O Thou destroyer of misery, Thou alone dost exist eternally, and none besides. Therefore I take refuge in Thee, the supreme Lord.

एकः कर्ता त्वं हि सर्वस्य शम्भो
नानारूपोऽप्येकरूपस्वरूपः ।
यद्वत् प्रत्यप्स्वर्के एकोऽप्यनेकः
तस्मान्नान्यं त्वां विनेशं प्रपद्ये ॥ १२१ ॥

Skandapurana, IV, Pt. I, Ch. X, 27.

रज्जौ सर्पः शुक्तिकायां च रूप्यं
नीरं पुरस्तान्मृगाल्ये मरीचौ ।
यद्वत्तद्वद्विश्वगेषं प्रपञ्चो
यस्मिन् ज्ञाते तं प्रपद्ये महेशम् ॥ १२२ ॥

Skandapurana, IV, Pt. I, Ch. X, 128.

नो वेद स्वामीश साक्षाद्धि वेद
नो वा विष्णुर्नो विधाताऽखिलस्य ।
नो योगीन्द्रा नेन्द्रमुख्याश्च देवा
भक्तो वेद त्वामतस्त्वां प्रपद्ये ॥ १२३ ॥

Skandapurana, IV, Pt. I, Ch. X, 131.

121. O Thou bestower of well-being, Thou art the sole creator of all. Assuming various forms Thou art yet one and immutable. Though one, Thou dost appear as many just as the sun is reflected in various waters. Therefore to Thee, the great God, do I turn for refuge, and to none else.

122. I take refuge in the supreme Lord, who being realised, the notion of this entire phenomenal existence appears as unreal as that of the snake in the rope, of silver in the mother-of-pearl, and of water ahead in the mirage.

123. O Lord, the Vedas have not any direct knowledge of Thee, nor hath the preserver of the universe, nor the creator, nor even the greatest of Yogins, nor the gods and their chief. Thou art known to Thy devotee alone. Therefore my God, do I take refuge in Thee.

नो ते गोत्रं नापि जन्मापि नाख्या

नो वा रूपं नैव शीलं न देश: ।

इत्थम्भूतोऽपीश्वरस्त्वं त्रिलोक्या:

सर्वान् कामान् पूरयेस्तद्भजे त्वाम् ॥ १२४ ॥

Skandapurana, IV, Pt. I, Ch. X 132:

त्वमेव विष्णुश्चतुराननस्त्वं

त्वमेव मृत्युर्धनदस्त्वमेव ।

त्वमेव सूक्ष्म: पुरुषोऽव्ययस्त्वं

त्वमेव सूक्ष्मात् परमं च सूक्ष्मम् ॥ १२५ ॥

Skandapurana Nilakanthastava, 52.

व्यक्तिस्त्वमेव प्रकृतिस्त्वमेव

त्वमेव भूमि: सलिलं त्वमेव ।

त्वमेव वह्नि: पवनस्त्वमेव

त्वमेव यज्ञो नियमस्त्वमेव ॥ १२६ ॥

Skandapurana Nilakanthastava, 53.

124. My Lord, Thou hast no lineage, nor birth, nor name, nor form. Neither hast Thou any duty nor any locality. Still Thou art the Lord of all the worlds, and Thou dost fulfil all desires. Therefore, my God, do I take refuge in Thee.

125. O Lord, Thou art the all-pervading Deity and the creator sublime. Thou art Death and the giver of wealth. Thou art the Spirit dwelling in all, invisible and immutable. Thou art the subtlest of the subtle.

126. Thou art the manifest and the unmanifest. Thou art the earth, water, fire and air. Thou art the sacrifice and the rules thereof.

त्वमेव भूतं भवनञ्च भव्यं
    त्वमेव सर्वे: प्रकरोषि धर्मम् ।
त्वमेव सर्वस्य चराचरस्य
पृथग्विभक्ता प्रलये च गोप्ता ॥ १२७ ॥

Skandapurana, Nilakanthastava, 54.

127. Thou art the past, present and future. Thou art the All. Thou art the mighty revealer of religion. Thou alone didst create diverse things, both moving and non-moving. Thou again art their preserver during dissolution.

UNIVERSAL PRAYERS

FROM PURANAS Etc.

PART II

त्वं ब्रह्म परमं धाम निरीहो निरहङ्कृतिः ।
निर्गुणश्च निराकारः साकारस्सगुणस्स्वयम् ॥ १२८ ॥

Brahmavaivartapurana, IV, xviii, 36.

साक्षिरूपश्च निर्लिप्तः परमात्मा निराकृतिः ।
प्रकृतिः पुरुषस्त्वं च कारणं च तयोः परम ॥ १२९ ॥

Brahmavaivartapurana, IV, xviii, 37.

सर्वशक्तीश्वरस्सर्वैः सर्वशक्त्याश्रयस्सदा ।
त्वमनीहः स्वयञ्ज्योतिः सर्वानन्दस्सनातनः ॥ १३० ॥

Brahmavaivartapurana, IV, xviii, 42.

वयं किं स्तवनं कुर्मः स्त्रियः प्राणेश्वरेश्वर ।
प्रसन्नो भव नो देव दीनबन्धो कृपां कुरु ॥ १३१ ॥

Brahmavaivartapurana, IV, xviii, 46.

128.   O Lord, Thou art Brahman, the highest goal, without desire and without egotism.   Thou art without attributes and without forms.   Yet dost Thou possess attributes and forms.

129.   Thou art the supreme Being, the witness unattached and formless.   Thou art primal matter and soul, and Thou art the primal cause of them both.

130.   Thou art everything.   Thou art the controller of all powers and the source of all powers.   Thou art devoid of desires. Thou verily art the self luminous, all-blissful, eternal Being.

131.   O lord and master of our souls, what praise can we offer to Thee ? O Lord, do Thou condescend to favour us with Thy grace.   Thou art the friend and guide of the needy.   Have mercy on us.

जगद्गुरो नमस्तुभ्यं शिवाय शिवदाय च ।
योगीन्द्राणां च योगीन्द्र गुरूणां गुरवे नमः ॥१३२॥

Brahmavaivartapurana, IV, xxx, 43.

मृत्योर्मृत्युस्वरूपेण मृत्युसंसारखण्डन ।
मृत्योरीश मृत्युबीज मृत्युञ्जय नमोऽस्तु ते ॥१३३॥

Brahmavaivartapurana, IV, xxx, 44.

कालरूपं कलयतां कालकालेश कारण ।
कालादतीत कालस्थ कालकाल नमोऽस्तु ते ॥१३४॥

Brahmavaivartapurana, IV, xxx, 45.

गुणातीत गुणाधार गुणबीज गुणात्मक ।
गुणीश गुणिनां बीज गुणिनां गुरवे नमः ॥ १३५॥

Brahmavaivartapurana, IV, xxx, 46.

132. Salutations unto Thee, O teacher of the universe. Thou art the Lord auspicious and the giver of bliss, the foremost of the perfect Yogis, the teacher of teachers. Salutations unto Thee.

133. Thou art the death of death, the saviour in the world of death, the lord of death, the cause of death and the conqueror of death. Salutations unto Thee.

134. Of measurers Thou art Time; Thou art the lord of Time, the origin of Time. Thou art beyond Time and yet Thou abidest in Time. O Thou destroyer of all destroyers, salutations to Thee.

135. Thou art the One beyond all attributes, yet Thou supportest them all. Thou art the origin of all attributes and abidest in them as their Self. Thou art the lord of those who possess noble attributes. Thou art also their progenitor and teacher. Salutations to Thee.

ब्रह्मस्वरूप ब्रह्मज्ञ ब्रह्मभावे च तत्पर ।
ब्रह्मबीजस्वरूपेण जगद्बीज नमोऽस्तु ते ॥ १३६ ॥

Brahmavaivartapurana, IV, xxx, 47.

यस्मात्सर्वमिदं प्रपञ्चरचितं मायाजगज्जायते
यस्मिंस्तिष्ठति याति चान्तसमये कल्पानुकल्पे
पुनः ।
यं ध्यात्वा मुनयः प्रपञ्चरहितं विन्दन्ति मोक्षं ध्रुवं
तं वन्दे पुरुषोत्तमाख्यममलं नित्यं विभुं
निश्चलम् ॥ १३७ ॥

Brahmapurana, Chapter I.

136. Thou verily art Brahman, the knower of Brahman, the constant possessor of the consciousness of Brahman. Thou art Brahman, the ultimate cause. Salutations to Thee from whom the universe has sprung.

137. Adoration unto the supreme Being, pure, eternal and all-pervading, the changeless Reality, the one Being, meditating upon whom sages attain liberation, eternal and undifferentiated; the One out of whom the visible world, the scene of diversity, comes into existence, in whom it rests, and to whom it returns in the end when the world-cycles come to a close.

यं ध्यायन्ति बुधाः समाधिसमये शुद्धं वियत्सन्निभम्
नित्यानन्दमयं प्रसन्नममलं सर्वेश्वरं निर्गुणम् ।
व्यक्ताव्यक्तपरं प्रपञ्चरहितं ध्यानैकगम्यं विभुं
तं संसारविनाशहेतुमजरं वन्दे हरिं मुक्तिदम् ॥

Brahmapurana, Chapter I.

यं न जानन्ति श्रुतयो यं न जानन्ति सूरयः ।
तं नमामि जगद्धेतुं मायिनं तममायिनम् ॥ १३९ ॥

Padmapurana.

यो देवस्त्यक्तसञ्ज्ञानां शान्तानां करुणार्णवः ।
करोति ह्यात्मना सञ्ज्ञं तं वन्दे सञ्जवर्जितम् ॥ १४० ॥

Padmapurana.

138. Adoration unto the Lord, the destroyer of all worldliness and bestower of salvation, the undecaying and infinite Being, the One who is attainable through meditation alone, who is free from illusion, and beyond the manifest and the unmanifest; the One who is of the form of bliss eternal, who is gracious, taintless, and without any attributes, who is the overlord; the One who is pure and limitless like the ether, and who is contemplated in Samadhi by the wise.

139. I salute Him who is the cause of the universe, who is unknown to the scriptures as well as to the learned, and who, though endowed with Maya—the divine Power—is still unaffected by it.

140. I salute the divine Being, the ocean of mercy, who associates in spirit with the unattached and the even-minded, and yet remains free from all taint of attachment.

9

यत्पादाब्जजलक्लिन्नसेवार्ज्जितमस्तका: ।
अवापु: परमां सिद्धिं तं वन्दे सर्ववन्दितम् ॥१४१॥

Padmapurana.

सर्वज्ञे सर्ववरदे सर्वदुष्टभयङ्करि ।
सर्वदु:खहरे देवि महालक्ष्मि नमोऽस्तु ते ॥ १४२ ॥

Mahalakshmyashtaka, 3.

सिद्धिबुद्धिप्रदे देवि मुक्तिमुक्तिप्रदायिनि ।
मन्त्रमूर्ते सदा देवि महालक्ष्मि नमोऽस्तु ते ॥१४३॥

Mahalakshmyashtaka, 4.

आद्यन्तरहिते देवि आद्यशक्ति महेश्वरि ।
योगजे योगसम्भूते महालक्ष्मि नमोऽस्तु ते ॥१४४॥

Mahalakshmyashtaka 5.

141. I salute Him, the adored of all, by the devoted worship of whose lotus feet, men with their foreheads drenched with the waters thereof, do attain the highest goal.

142. O Mother, Thou knowest all, Thou givest boons to all, Thou art a terror to the wicked, and Thou art the remover of the misery of all. O Mother auspicious, I bow to Thee.

143. O Mother divine, Thou art the giver of success and intelligence. Thou art the giver of both worldly enjoyment and liberation. The mystic sound symbols— the Mantras—verily constitute Thy form. Mother auspicious, I bow to Thee always.

144. O Mother supreme, Thou art without beginning and end. Thou art the primal Power. Thou art born of Yoga, and Thou art manifest through Yoga. O Mother auspicious, I bow to Thee.

स्थूलसूक्ष्मे महारौद्रे महाशक्ति महोदरे ।
महापापहरे देवि महालक्ष्मि नमोऽस्तु ते ॥ १४५ ॥

Mahalakshmyashtaka, 6.

पद्मासनस्थिते देवि परब्रह्मस्वरूपिणि ।
परमेशि जगन्मातर्महालक्ष्मि नमोऽस्तु ते ॥ १४६ ॥

Mahalakshmyashtaka, 7.

देव्या यया ततमिदं जगदात्मशक्त्या
    निःशेषदेवगणशक्तिसमूहमूर्त्या ।
तामम्बिकामखिलदेवमहर्षिपूज्यां
भक्त्या नताः स्म विदधातु शुभानि सा नः ॥१४७॥

Markandeyapurana, Devimahatmya, IV, 3.

145. Thou art both gross and subtle, most terrible and powerful. Thou containest all things, Thou removest even the greatest sins. O Mother auspicious, I bow to Thee.

146. Thou dwellest in the hearts of devotees, Thou verily art the supreme Brahman. Thou art also the supreme sovereign and mother of the universe. O Mother auspicious, I bow to Thee.

147. O divine Mother, Thine energy pervades this entire universe. Thou embodiest the powers of diverse presiding deities, Thou art the object of worship to all the gods and sages. Do Thou bestow on us what is auspicious. We bow down to Thee in devotion.

या श्री: स्वयं सुकृतिनां भवनेष्वलक्ष्मी:
पापात्मनां कृतधियां हृदयेषु बुद्धि: ।
श्रद्धा सतां कुलजनप्रभवस्य लज्जा
तां त्वां नता: स्म परिपालय देवि विश्वम् ॥१४८॥

Devimahatmya, IV, 5.

हेतु: समस्तजगतां त्रिगुणापि दोषै-
र्नज्ञायसे हरिहरादिभिरप्यपारा ।
सर्वाश्रयाखिलमिदं जगदंशभूत-
मव्याकृता हि परमा प्रकृतिस्त्वमाद्या ॥ १४९ ॥

Devimahatmya, IV, 7.

या मुक्तिहेतुरविचिन्त्यमहाव्रता त्व-
मभ्यस्यसे सुनियतेन्द्रियतत्त्वसारै: ।
मोक्षार्थिभिर्मुनिभिरस्तसमस्तदोषै-
र्विद्याडसि सा भगवती परमा हि देवी ॥१५०॥

Devimahatmya, IV, 9.

148. Thou art good fortune itself in the dwellings of the virtuous and ill-fortune in those of the sinful. Thou art intelligence in the intelligent, faith in the heart of the devotee, and modesty in the high-born. We bow to Thee. Do Thou, O Mother, protect this universe.

149. Thou art the cause of all the worlds. Thou art endowed with the primordial Energy which produces the phenomenon, yet Thou art known to be transcendent and faultless. Incomprehensible Thou art even to the greatest of the gods. Thou art the refuge of all. The whole world is but a part of Thee. Thou art the unmanifest, primordial, supreme Creatrix.

150. O Mother divine, Thy virtues are inscrutable. Thou art the supreme knowledge, the cause of liberation. Thou art sought after by the sages, who are eager for salvation, who have fully controlled their senses, and who are free from all faults.

या देवी सर्वभूतेषु विष्णुमायेति शब्दिता ।
नमस्तस्यै नमस्तस्यै नमस्तस्यै नमो नमः ॥ १५१ ॥

Devimahatmya, V, 14.

या देवी सर्वभूतेषु चेतनेत्यभिधीयते ।
नमस्तस्यै नमस्तस्यै नमस्तस्यै नमो नमः ॥ १५२ ॥

Devimahatmya, V, 15.

या देवी सर्वभूतेषु शक्तिरूपेण संस्थिता ।
नमस्तस्यै नमस्तस्यै नमस्तस्यै नमो नमः ॥ १५३ ॥

Devimahatmya, V, 20

या देवी सर्वभूतेषु क्षान्तिरूपेण संस्थिता ।
नमस्तस्यै नमस्तस्यै नमस्तस्यै नमो नमः ॥ १५४ ॥

Devimahatmya, V, 22.

या देवी सर्वभूतेषु शान्तिरूपेण संस्थिता ।
नमस्तस्यै नमस्तस्यै नमस्तस्यै नमो नमः ॥ १५५ ॥

Devimahatmya, V, 25.

151. Salutations to the divine mother, the Lord's own Maya—the inscrutable Power—pervading all things. Salutations to Her, salutations to Her, salutations, salutations.

152. Salutations to the divine Mother, who is known as intelligence in all beings. Salutations to Her, salutations to Her, salutations, salutations.

153. Salutations to the divine Mother, who exists in all beings in the form of power. Salutations to Her, salutations to Her, salutations, salutations.

154. Salutations to the divine Mother, who exists in all beings as forgiveness. Salutations to Her, salutations to Her, salutations, salutations.

155. Salutations to the divine Mother, who exists in all beings in the form of peace. Salutations to Her, salutations to Her, salutations, salutations.

या देवी सर्वभूतेषु श्रद्धारूपेण संस्थिता ।
नमस्तस्यै नमस्तस्यै नमस्तस्यै नमो नमः ॥ १५६ ॥

Devimahatmya, V, 26.

या देवी सर्वभूतेषु कान्तिरूपेण संस्थिता ।
नमस्तस्यै नमस्तस्यै नमस्तस्यै नमो नमः ॥ १५७ ॥

Devimahatmya, V, 27.

या देवी सर्वभूतेषु दयारूपेण संस्थिता ।
नमस्तस्यै नमस्तस्यै नमस्तस्यै नमो नमः ॥ १५८ ॥

Devimahatmya, V, 31.

या देवी सर्वभूतेषु मातृरूपेण संस्थिता ।
नमस्तस्यै नमस्तस्यै नमस्तस्यै नमो नमः ॥ १५९ ॥

Devimahatmya, V, 32.

इन्द्रियाणामधिष्ठात्री भूतानां चाखिलेषु या ।
भूतेषु सततं तस्यै व्याप्त्यै देव्यै नमो नमः ॥ १६० ॥

Devimahatmya, Chapter V, 35.

156. Salutations to the divine Mother, who exists in all beings in the form of faith. Salutations to Her, salutations to Her, salutations, salutations.

157. Salutations to the divine Mother, who exists in all beings in the form of beauty. Salutations to Her, salutations to Her, salutations, salutations.

158. Salutations to the divine Mother, who exists in all beings in the form of mercy. Salutations to Her, salutations to Her, salutations, salutations.

159. Salutations to the divine Mother, who exists in all beings as the Mother. Salutations to Her, salutations to Her, salutations, salutations.

160. Salutations to the divine Mother, who is the presiding deity of all the senses, who exists in all beings and pervades all things. Salutations to Her, salutations to Her, salutations, salutations.

चितिरूपेण या कृत्स्नमेतद्व्याप्य स्थिता जगत् ।
नमस्तस्यै नमस्तस्यै नमस्तस्यै नमो नम: ॥ १६१ ॥

Devimahatmya, V, 36.

देवि प्रपन्नार्तिहरे प्रसीद

प्रसीद मातर्जगतोऽखिलस्य ।

प्रसीद विश्वेश्वरि पाहि विश्वं

त्वमीश्वरी देवि चराचरस्य ॥ १६२ ॥

Devimahatmya, XI, 2.

त्वं वैष्णवी शक्तिरनन्तवीर्या

विश्वस्य बीजं परमासि माया ।

सम्मोहितं देवि समस्तमेतत्

त्वं वै प्रसन्ना भुवि मुक्तिहेतु: ॥ १६३ ॥

Devimahatmya, XI, 4.

161.   Salutations to the divine Mother who, pervading all the world, exists therein in the form of consciousness.   Salutations to Her, salutations to Her, salutations, salutations.

162.   O Mother, Thou art the destroyer of the troubles of Thy suppliants, Thou art the mother of the universe. Let Thy mercy be upon all. O Mother, Thou art the mistress of the universe. Thou art the one ruler of the moving and non-moving. Do Thou protect the universe and shower Thy mercy on all.

163.   O Mother, Thou art the great primal Energy, the source of infinite strength.   Thou art the seed of the world, and illusion divine. Thou hast enchanted the whole universe, O Goddess supreme, by Thy deluding charms.   And yet being propitious, Thou bestowest salvation upon men.

विद्याः समस्तास्तव देवि भेदाः

स्त्रियः समस्ताः सकला जगत्सु ।

त्वयैकया पूरितमम्बयैतत्

का ते स्तुतिः स्तव्यपरापरोक्तिः ॥ १६४ ॥

Devimahatmya, XI, 5.

सर्वभूता यदा देवि भुक्तिमुक्तिप्रदायिनी ।

त्वं स्तुता स्तुतये का वा भवन्तु परमोक्तयः ॥१६५॥

Devimahatmya, XI, 6.

सर्वमङ्गलमाङ्गल्ये शिवे सर्वार्थसाधिके ।

शरण्ये त्र्यम्बके गौरि नारायणि नमोऽस्तुते ॥ १६६ ॥

Devimahatmya, XI, 9.

सृष्टिस्थितिविनाशानां शक्तिभूते सनातनि ।

गुणाश्रये ऽगुणमये नारायणि नमोऽस्तु ते ॥ १६७ ॥

Devimahatmya, XI, 10.

164. All sciences come from Thee, and all women in all the world are parts of Thee. By Thee alone, O Mother, is the universe filled. How can we praise Thee? Art Thou not beyond the reach of the highest praise?

165. Thou, O Mother, dost exist as all things. Being worshipped, Thou bestowest heaven and liberation. What words, however sublime, can suffice for Thy praise?

166. O auspicious One, Thou art the source of all auspiciousness. Thou art the accomplisher of all cherished desires. Thou art the giver of refuge. Thou possessest the eye of wisdom and beautiful form. O Thou Power divine, salutations to Thee.

167. O eternal One, Thou art the energy of creation, maintenance, and destruction. Thou art the abode of different modes of energy and art yet beyond them. O Thou Power divine, salutations to Thee.

शरणागतदीनार्तपरित्राणपरायणे ।
सर्वस्यार्तिहरे देवि नारायणि नमोऽस्तु ते ॥ १६८ ॥

Devimahatmya, XI, 11.

सर्वस्वरूपे सर्वेशे सर्वशक्तिसमन्विते ।
भयेभ्यस्त्राहि नो देवि दुर्गे देवि नमोऽस्तु ते ॥ १६९ ॥

Devimahatmya, XI, 23.

नमो विश्वप्रबोधाय नमो भ्राजिष्णुजिष्णवे ।
ज्योतिषे च नमस्तुभ्यं ज्ञानार्काय नमो नमः ॥ १७० ॥

Bhavishyapurana.

नमस्त्रैलोक्यनाथाय भूतानां पतये नमः ।
नमः कैवल्यनाथाय नमस्ते दिव्यचक्षुषे ॥ १७१ ॥

Bhavishyapurana.

168. O Mother, Thou art the saviour of the distressed and of the care-worn, who take refuge in Thee. Thou art the remover of the misery of all. O Thou Power divine, salutations to Thee.

169. O Mother, Thou art in the form of all things. Thou dost control all. Thou art the embodiment of all power, do Thou protect us from all fear. O remover of all ills, salutations to Thee.

170. Salutations to Thee, the awakener of the universe. Salutations to Thee, the resplendent and the glorious. Salutations to Thee, the Being effulgent. Salutations to Thee, the light of knowledge.

171. Salutations to Thee, the lord of the worlds. Salutations to Thee, the lord of all beings. Salutations to Thee, the lord of salvation. Salutations to Thee, the possessor of divine vision.

10

त्वं ज्योतिस्त्वं द्युतिर्ब्रह्मा त्वं विष्णुस्त्वं प्रजापतिः ।
त्वमेव रुद्रो रुद्रात्मा वायुरग्निस्त्वमेव च ॥ १७२ ॥

Bhavishyapurana.

अग्रतश्च नमस्तुभ्यं पृष्ठतश्च सदा नमः ।
पार्श्वतश्च नमस्तुभ्यं नमस्ते चास्तु सर्वदा ॥ १७३ ॥

Bhavishyapurana.

नमो वेदान्तवेद्याय सर्वकर्मादिसाक्षिणे ।
नमो हरितवर्णाय सुवर्णाय नमो नमः ॥ १७४ ॥

Bhavishyapurana.

हृदयकमलमध्ये निर्विशेषं निरीहं
    हरिहरविधिवेद्यं योगिभिर्ध्यानगम्यम् ।
जननमरणभीतिभ्रंशिसच्चित्स्वरूपं
    सकलभुवनबीजं ब्रह्म चैतन्यमीडे ॥ १७५ ॥

Mahanirvanatantra, III, 50.

172. Thou art the creator and protector of the universe. Thou art the lord of beings. Thou art the destroyer with terrible powers. Thou art the God of wind and also the God of fire.

173. Salutations to Thee who art before. Always salutations to Thee who art behind, salutations to Thee who art on every side. At all times salutations unto Thee.

174. Salutations to Thee, the One to be known through the Vedanta, the primeval witness of all activities. Salutations to Thee who shines through different colours.

175. In the lotus of my heart do I contemplate the divine Intelligence, the Brahman without distinction and difference, who is the object of realisation to even the creator, protector and destroyer of the universe; whom the Yogis attain through meditation; who destroys the fear of birth and death; and who is existence, intelligence, and the seed of all the worlds.

नमस्ते सते सर्वलोकाश्रयाय

नमस्ते चिते विश्वरूपात्मकाय ।

नमोऽद्वैततत्त्वाय मुक्तिप्रदाय

नमो ब्रह्मणे व्यापिने निर्गुणाय ॥ १७६ ॥

Mahanirvanatantra, III, 59.

त्वमेकं शरण्यं त्वमेकं वरेण्यं

त्वमेकं जगत्पालकं स्वप्रकाशम् ।

त्वमेकं जगत्कर्तृपातृप्रहर्तृ

त्वमेकं परं निश्चलं निर्विकल्पम् ॥ १७७ ॥

Mahanirvanatantra, III, 60.

भयानां भयं भीषणं भीषणानां

गतिः प्राणिनां पावनं पावनानाम् ।

महोच्चैः पदानां नियन्तृ त्वमेकं

परेषां परं रक्षणं रक्षणानाम् ॥ १७८ ॥

Mahanirvanatantra, III, 61.

176. Salutations to Thee, the existence absolute, the support of all the worlds. Salutations to Thee, the intelligence absolute, who dost appear as the universe. Salutations to Thee the one Reality without a second, the giver of salvation. Salutations to Thee, the Brahman, the all-pervading, the absolute.

177. Thou art the only refuge, the only object of adoration, the one ruler of the universe, the Being self-effulgent. Thou alone art the creator, preserver and destroyer of the universe. Thou art the highest, the immovable, the absolute.

178. O Lord, Thou art the dread of even the dreadful, the terror of the terrible, the refuge of all beings, the purifier of all purifiers. Thou alone art the ruler of even the high-placed ones. Thou art the supreme over the supreme, the protector of the protectors.

परेश प्रभो सर्वरूपाविनाशिन्
   अनिर्देश्य सर्वेन्द्रियागम्य सत्य ।
अचिन्त्याक्षर व्यापकाव्यक्ततत्व
   जगद्व्रासकाधीश पायादपायात् ॥ १७९ ॥

Mahanirvanatantra, III, 62.

तदेकं स्मरामस्तदेकं भजाम-
   स्तदेकं जगत्साक्षिरूपं नमामः ।
सदेकं निधानं निरालंबमीशं
   भवाम्भोधिपोतं शरण्यं व्रजामः ॥ १८० ॥

Mahanirvanatantra. III, 63.

नमस्ते परमं ब्रह्म नमस्ते परमात्मने ।
निर्गुणाय नमस्तुभ्यं सद्रूपाय नमो नमः ॥ १८१ ॥

Mahanirvanatantra, III, 74.

179. O Lord supreme, Thou art the imperishable, undefinable Being, yet Thou appearest as all things. Thou art imperceptible to the senses, yet art Thou the very Truth, incomprehensible and immutable. Thou art the all-pervading, hidden essence. Lord and Light of the world, do Thou save us from harm.

180. On Thee, the One, alone we meditate. To Thee, the One, alone we offer our worship. To Thee, the One, alone, who art the witness of the universe, do we tender our salutations. In Thee, the One, alone, who art our sole support, and the self-existent Lord, the vessel of safety in the ocean of existence, do we seek refuge.

181. I bow to Thee, the supreme Brahman. I bow to Thee, the supreme Self. I bow to Thee who art above all qualities. I bow to Thee, the ever-existent, again and again.

गुरुर्ब्रह्मा गुरुर्विष्णुर्गुरुर्देवो महेश्वरः ।
गुरुरेव परं ब्रह्म तस्मै श्रीगुरवे नमः ॥ १८२ ॥

Visvasaratantra.

अज्ञानतिमिरान्धस्य ज्ञानाञ्जनशलाकया ।
चक्षुरुन्मीलितं येन तस्मै श्रीगुरवे नमः ॥ १८३ ॥

Visvasaratantra.

अखण्डमण्डलाकारं व्याप्तं येन चराचरम् ।
तत् पदं दर्शितं येन तस्मै श्रीगुरवे नमः ॥ १८४ ॥

Visvasaratantra.

चिन्मयं व्यापितं सर्वं त्रैलोक्यं सचराचरम् ।
तत्पदं दर्शितं येन तस्मै श्रीगुरवे नमः ॥ १८५ ॥

Visvasaratantra.

182. The Guru (preceptor) is no other than Brahmā, the creator. The Guru is no other than Vishnu, the preserver. The Guru is no other than the great God Siva, the destroyer. The Guru is verily Brahman Itself. To the divine Guru I bow.

183. I bow to the divine Guru, who by the application of the collyrium of knowledge, opens the eyes of one blinded by the disease of ignorance.

184. I bow to the divine Guru, who reveals to one the divine Being that encircles and permeates the moving and the non-moving.

185. I bow to the divine Guru by whom is revealed the divine Being, the intelligence absolute, that permeates all the worlds with all their objects, moving and non-moving.

अनेकजन्मसम्प्राप्तकर्मबन्धविदाहिने ।
आत्मज्ञानप्रदानेन तस्मै श्रीगुरवे नमः ॥ १८६ ॥

Visvasaratantra.

मन्त्रनाथः श्रीजगन्नाथो मद्गुरुः श्रीजगद्गुरुः ।
ममात्मा सर्वभूतात्मा तस्मै श्रीगुरवे नमः ॥ १८७ ॥

Visvasaratantra.

ब्रह्मानन्दं परमसुखदं केवलं ज्ञानमूर्तिं
द्वन्द्वातीतं गगनसदृशं तत्त्वमस्यादिलक्ष्यम् ।
एकं नित्यं विमलमचलं सर्वधीसाक्षिभूतं
भावातीतं त्रिगुणरहितं सद्गुरुं तं नमामि ॥ १८८ ॥

Visvasaratantra.

186. I bow to the divine Guru who imparts to the disciple the fire of self-knowledge, and burns away his bonds of Karma accumulated through many births.

187. I bow to the true divine Guru. He, my Lord, is the Lord of the universe. He, my Guru, is the Guru of the universe. He, my Self, is the Self of the universe.

188. I bow to the Guru who is the embodiment of the bliss of Brahman, the giver of the greatest beatitude, the absolute, the personification of the highest knowledge; who is beyond the pairs of opposites (like pleasure and pain) and untouched by evil, like the sky; whom " Thou art That " and similar scriptural passages have in view; the One without a second, the eternal, the pure, the immovable, the witness of all mental modifications, abiding ever beyond thoughts and attributes.

नित्यं शुद्धं निराकारं निराभासं निरञ्जनम् ।
नित्यबोधं चिदानन्दं गुरुं ब्रह्म नमाम्यहम् ॥ १८९ ॥

Visvasaratantra.

नमस्ते शरण्ये शिवे सानुकम्पे
    नमस्ते जगद्व्यापिके विश्वरूपे ।
नमस्ते जगद्वन्द्यपादारविन्दे
    नमस्ते जगत्तारिणि त्राहि दुर्गे ॥ १९० ॥

Visvasaratantra.

नमस्ते जगच्चिन्त्यमानस्वरूपे
    नमस्ते महायोगिनि ज्ञानरूपे ।
नमस्ते सदानन्दनन्दस्वरूपे
    नमस्ते जगत्तारिणि त्राहि दुर्गे ॥ १९१ ॥

Visvasaratantra.

189. I bow to the Guru, the Brahman, eternal, pure and formless, self-effulgent, taintless, ever awake and of the nature of intelligence and bliss.

190. O Mother divine, Thou art the remover of the miseries of the devotees. Thou art the eternal refuge, ever blissful and ever compassionate; to Thee I bow. Thou pervadest the whole universe and assumest the cosmic form; to Thee I bow. Thy lotus feet the whole universe worships; to Thee I bow. Thou art the saviour of the universe. Do Thou protect us. To Thee I bow.

191. Thou art the saviour of the universe; do Thou protect us. To Thee I bow. O Mother divine, Thy true form is the object of meditation for the whole world. To Thee I bow Thou art the embodiment of the highest Yoga and knowledge. Thou art the delight of the ever-blissful Lord. To Thee I bow. Thou art the saviour of the universe, do Thou protect us. To Thee I bow.

अनाथस्य दीनस्य तृष्णातुरस्य

भयार्तस्य भीतस्य बद्धस्य जन्तो: ।

त्वमेका गतिर्देवि निस्तारदात्रि

नमस्ते जगत्तारिणि त्राहि दुर्गे ॥ १९२ ॥

Visvasaratantra.

ध्यायन्ते योगिनो योगात् सिद्धा: सिद्धेश्वराश्च यम् ।

तं ध्याये सततं शुद्धं भगवन्तं सनातनम् ॥

सेवे तं सततं सन्तो ब्रह्मेशशेषसंज्ञका: ।

सेवन्ते निर्गुणं ब्रह्म भगवन्तं सनातनम् ॥

॥ १९३-१९४ ॥

Naradapancharatra, Part I, Ch. XII.

निर्लिप्तं च निरीहं च परमात्मानमीश्वरम् ।

नित्यं सत्यं च परमं भगवन्तं सनातनम् ॥

सर्गाणामादिभूतं च सर्वबीजं परात्परम् ।

योगिनस्तं प्रपद्यन्ते भगवन्तं सनातनम् ॥

॥ १९५-१९६ ॥

Naradapancharatra, Part I, Ch. XII.

192. O Mother, the remover of the miseries of the devotees, Thou art the saviour of the poor and the helpless. Thou art the protector of those oppressed by desire and stricken with fear. Thou art the refuge of the afflicted and the bound. Thou art, O mother, the goal and the giver of emancipation. Thou art the saviour of the universe; do Thou protect us. To Thee I bow.

193-194. Always do I meditate on that supreme Being who is eternal and pure, and who is meditated upon by the adepts, super-adepts and Yogins. I always serve that Lord eternal, who is the attribute-less Brahman served by the creator and the destroyer of the universe and other gods.

195-196. The eternal Lord is without attachment and desires. He is the supreme Spirit, the highest God, Truth unchangeable, and supreme. He is realised by the Yogins as the origin of creation, as the seed of all, as the one greater than the greatest.

बीजं नानावताराणां सर्वकारणकारकम् ।

वेदावेद्यं वेदबीजं वेदकारणकारकम् ॥

योगिनो यं प्रपद्यन्ते तं प्रपद्ये सनातनम् ॥ १९७ ॥

Naradapancharatra, Part I, Ch. XII

सर्वभूतात्मभूतस्थं सर्वाधारं सनातनम् ।

सर्वकारणकर्तारं निदानं प्रकृतेः परम् ॥

निरामयं निराभासं निरवद्यं निरञ्जनम् ।

नित्यानन्दं निराकारमद्वैतं तमसः परम् ॥

परात्परतरं तत्त्वं सत्यानन्दं चिदात्मकम् ।

मनसा शिरसा नित्यं प्रणमामि रघूत्तमम् ॥

॥ १९८-२०० ॥

Sanatkumarasamhita.

माता पिता तथा भ्राता त्वमेव रघुवल्लभ ।

सर्वेषां त्वं परं ब्रह्म त्वन्मयं सर्वमेव हि ॥ २०१ ॥

Sanatkumarasamhita.

197.   I take refuge in the eternal Lord,
who is the refuge of the Yogins, who is
the seed of all Incarnations and the cause
of all causes, who is unknowable by the
Vedas, the seed of the Vedas and the source
of the cause of the Vedas.

198-200.   O blissful Lord, Thou art
the Self of all beings, the support of all,
the eternal, the cause of all causes, beyond
the bounds of Nature.   Thou art pure and
self-effulgent, without blemish and without
taint.   Thou art bliss eternal, without form
and duality, and beyond all darkness.   Thou
art greater than the greatest, truth absolute,
the very embodiment of existence, bliss
and intelligence.   To Thee I bow down
with my whole heart.

201.   O Lord, Thou art the mother,
father and brother of all.   Thou art the
supreme Brahman, and all things are manifestations of Thee.

11

त्वमक्षरं परं ज्योतिस्त्वमेव पुरुषोत्तम ।
त्वमेव तारकं ब्रह्म त्वत्तोऽन्यन्नैव किञ्चन ॥ २०२ ॥

Sanatkumarasamhita.

शान्तं सर्वगतं सूक्ष्मं परं ब्रह्म सनातनम् ।
राजीवलोचनं रामं प्रणमामि जगत्पतिम् ॥ २०३ ॥

Sanatkumarasamhita.

अचिन्त्यापि साकारशक्तिस्वरूपा
    प्रतिव्यक्त्यधिष्ठानसत्त्वैकमूर्तिः ।
गुणातीतनिर्द्वन्द्वबोधैकगम्या
    त्वमेका परब्रह्मरूपेण सिद्धा ॥ २०४ ॥

Mahakalasamhita.

202. O supreme Being, Thou art the immutable and supreme light. Thou art the saviour, the Brahman. And there exists nothing but Thee.

203. Thou art the eternal Brahman, tranquil, all-pervading and subtle. To Thee do I bow down, O charming and blissful Lord of the Universe.

204. Mother, Thou art beyond comprehension, yet art Thou the embodiment of infinite power. Thou art present everywhere, and Thy existence is visible in every being. Thou art beyond all attributes and duality. Thou art attainable through the highest knowledge alone. Thou art the One without a second, known as the Brahman supreme.

न ते नामगोत्रे न ते जन्ममृत्यू
    न ते धामचेष्टे न ते दुःखसौख्ये ।
न ते मित्रशत्रू न ते बन्धमोक्षौ
    स्वमेका परब्रह्मरूपेण सिद्धा ॥ २०५ ॥

Mahakalasamhita.

न बाला न च त्वं वयःस्था न वृद्धा
    न च स्त्री न षण्डः पुमान्नैव च त्वम् ।
सुरो नासुरो नो नरो वा न नारी
    त्वमेका परब्रह्मरूपेण सिद्धा ॥ २०६ ॥

Mahakalasamhita.

यथा बिम्बमेकं रवेरम्बरस्थं
    प्रतिच्छायया तावदेकोदकेषु ।
समुद्रासतेऽनेकरूपं यथावत्
    त्वमेका परब्रह्मरूपेण सिद्धा ॥ २०७ ॥

Mahakalasamhita

205. Thou hast neither name, nor lineage; neither birth, nor death; neither abode, nor activity. Thou hast neither pain, nor pleasure; neither friend, nor enemy; neither bondage, nor freedom. Thou art the One without a second, known as the Brahman supreme.

206. Thou art neither a girl, nor a woman young or old. Thou art neither masculine nor feminine, neither female nor neuter. Thou art neither a god, nor a demon, nor a human being. Thou art the One without a second, known as the Brahman supreme.

207. As the one sun, reflected in different pools of water, appears as so many different suns, so Thou, too, O Mother, dost appear as many through delusion. But still Thou art the One without a second, known as the Brahman supreme.

स्वकर्मफलनिर्दिष्टां यां यां योनिं व्रजाम्यहम् ।
तस्यां तस्यां हृषीकेश त्वयि भक्तिर्दृढास्तु मे॥२०८॥

Prapanna Gita, 10.

नान्यद्वदामि न शृणोमि न चिन्तयामि
        नान्यत् स्मरामि न भजामि न चाश्रयामि ।
भक्त्या त्वदीयचरणाम्बुजमन्तरेण
        श्रीश्रीनिवास पुरुषोत्तम देहि दास्यम् ॥ २०९ ॥

Prapanna Gita, 26.

त्वमेव माता च पिता त्वमेव
        त्वमेव बन्धुश्च सखा त्वमेव ।
त्वमेव विद्या द्रविणं त्वमेव
        त्वमेव सर्वं मम देवदेव ॥ २१० ॥

Prapanna Gita, 28.

नाथ योनिसहस्रेषु येषु येषु व्रजाम्यहम् ।
तेषु तेष्वचला भक्तिरच्युतास्तु सदा त्वयि॥२११॥

Prapanna Gita, 41.

208. O Lord of the senses, may my
devotion to Thee remain firm, whatever
bodies I may obtain according to the fruits
of my work.

209. O Lord, Thou supreme Being, in
my devotion I shall not speak of, nor hear
of, nor think of, nor recall, nor adore, nor
resort to, anything other than Thy lotus
feet. O Thou the seat of all virtue and
majesty, vouchsafe unto me the privilege
of serving Thee.

210. Thou art my mother, Thou art
my father, Thou art my friend, Thou art
my comrade, Thou art my knowledge, Thou
art my wealth, Thou art my all-in-all, O
God of gods.

211. My Lord, should thousands of
births fall to my lot, may I still always
possess an unshakable and unflinching devotion to Thee.

या प्रीतिरविवेकानां विषयेष्वनपायिनी ।
त्वामनुस्मरतः सा मे हृदयान्माऽपसर्पतु ॥ २१२ ॥

Prapanna Gita, 42.

जानामि धर्मं न च मे प्रवृत्ति-
जानाम्यधर्मं न च मे निवृत्तिः ।
त्वया हृषीकेश हृदि स्थितेन
यथा नियुक्तोऽस्मि तथा करोमि ॥ २१३ ॥

Prapanna Gita, 57.

त्रयी सांख्यं योगः पशुपतिमतं वैष्णवमिति
प्रभिन्ने प्रस्थाने परमिदमदः पथ्यमिति च ।
रुचीनां वैचित्र्यादृजुकुटिलनानापथजुषां
नृणामेको गम्यस्त्वमसि पयसामर्णव इव ॥ २१४ ॥

Sivamahimnah Stotra, 7.

212.   May I think of Thee with that strong love which the ignorant cherish for the things of the world, and may that love never cease to abide in my heart.

213.   Lord, I know what virtue is, but I cannot practise it; I know what vice is, but I have no power to desist from it. Thou, O Lord of the senses, dwellest in my heart, and I do as Thou dost impel me to do.

214.   Different are the paths laid down in the Vedas, Sankhya, Yoga, and Shaiva and Vaishnava scriptures. Of these, some people take to one and some to another as the best. Devotees follow these diverse paths, straight or crooked, according to their different tendencies. Yet, O Lord, Thou alone art the ultimate goal of all men, as is the ocean is of all rivers.

नमो नेदिष्ठाय प्रियदव दविष्ठाय च नमो
नमः क्षोदिष्ठाय स्मरहर महिष्ठाय च नमः ।
नमो वर्षिष्ठाय त्रिनयन यविष्ठाय च नमो
नमःसर्वस्मै ते तदिदमतिसर्वाय च नमः॥ २१५ ॥

Sivamahimnah Stotra, 29.

बहुलरजसे विश्वोत्पत्तौ भवाय नमो नमः
प्रबलतमसे तत्संहारे हराय नमो नमः ।
जनसुखकृते सत्त्वस्थित्यै मृडाय नमो नमः
प्रमहसि पदे निस्त्रैगुण्ये शिवाय नमो नमः ॥

Sivamahimnah Stotra, 30.

215. Salutations to Thee, O Lord unattached, who art nearest and yet farthest.
Salutations to Thee, O destroyer of animal
passions, who art the smallest of the small
and yet art the greatest of the great.
Salutations to Thee, O possessor of the
highest wisdom, who art ancient and yet
ever youthful. Salutations to Thee who
art all things, seen and unseen, and yet
beyond them all.

216. Salutations to Thee, O Lord, who
as creator assumest the immense power of
dynamism (Rajas) and producest the universe. Salutations to Thee, who as destroyer causest its dissolution by the mighty
power of inertia (Tamas). Salutations to
Thee, who as protector blessest men with
happiness through the power of balance
(Sattva). Salutations to Thee, O auspicious Lord, who in Thy transcendent aspect
art again beyond the three qualities.

असितगिरिसमं स्यात् कज्जलं सिन्धुपात्रे

सुरतरुवरशाखा लेखनी पत्रमुर्वी ।

लिखति यदि गृहीत्वा शारदा सर्वकालं

तदपि तव गुणानामीश पारं न याति ॥२१७॥

Sivamahimnah Stotra, 32.

निबद्धमुग्धाञ्जलिरेष याचे

नीरन्ध्रदैन्योन्नतमुक्तकण्ठम् ।

दयाम्बुधे देव भवत्कटाक्ष-

दाक्षिण्यलेशेन सकृन्निषिञ्च ॥ २१८ ॥

Srikrishnakarnamrita, I, 30.

तमसि रविरिवोद्यन्मज्जतामम्बुराशौ

प्लव इव तृषितानां स्वादुवर्षीव मेघः ।

निधिरिव विधनानां दीर्घतीव्रामयानां

भिषगिव कुशलं नो दातुमायातु शौरिः ॥२१९॥

Srikrishnakarnamrita, III, 97.

217. If the goddess of learning were to write eternally, having the biggest branch of the celestial tree for Her pen, the whole earth for paper, the Blue Mountain for ink, and the ocean for the vessel thereof, even then, O Lord, Thy attributes cannot be fully described.

218. O Lord, with my palms folded together in all humility, and my voice rising high up in an unbroken stream of plaintive notes, I beseech Thee, O ocean of mercy, to bless me but once with the touch of the grace beaming from Thy glance.

219. Like the sun flashing forth light unto one enshrouded in darkness, like the boat rescuing a person sinking in the sea, like the cloud showering forth its refreshing waters on the thirsty, like the store-house of wealth removing the distress of the penniless, and like the physician bringing relief to a person suffering from a long and painful disease,—may He, the Lord, come and grant unto us what is auspicious.

प्रातः स्मरामि हृदि संस्फुरदात्मतत्वं
   सच्चित्सुखं परमहंसगतिं तुरीयम् ।
यत्स्वप्नजागरसुषुप्तमवैति नित्यं
   तद्ब्रह्म निष्कलमहं न च भूतसङ्घः ॥ २२० ॥

Sri Sankaracharya : Pratah-smarana Stotra, 1,

प्रातर्भजामि मनसो वचसामगम्यं
   वाचो विभान्ति निखिला यदनुग्रहेण ।
यन्नेति नेति वचनैर्निगमा अवोचु-
   स्तं देवदेवमजमच्युतमाहुरग्र्यम् ॥ २२१ ॥

Pratah-smarana Stotra, 2.

प्रातर्नमामि तमसः परमर्कवर्णं
   पूर्णं सनातनपदं पुरुषोत्तमाख्यम् ।
यस्मिन्निदं जगदशेषमशेषमूर्तौ
   रज्ज्वां भुजङ्गम इव प्रतिभासितं वै ॥ २२२ ॥

Pratah-smarana Stotra, 3.

220. At dawn I meditate within my heart on the self-effulgent Atman, the existence-knowledge-bliss Absolute, the goal of the greatest ascetics, the transcendent and the eternal, who is beyond the states of waking, dream and sleep. I am verily that indivisible Brahman, and not a combination of material elements.

221. At dawn I worship Him who is beyond the reach of mind and speech, but because of whose presence all speech becomes manifest. Him the scriptures indicate by the words " not this ", " not this " as beyond all attributes, Him the sages describe as the God of gods, eternal, immutable and supreme.

222. At dawn I salute the effulgent Being, who is beyond all darkness, who is called the supreme, the infinite and the eternal, in whom appears the world of manifold forms, like the snake superimposed on the rope.

विश्वं दर्पणदृश्यमाननगरीतुल्यं निजान्तर्गतं
    पश्यन्नात्मनि मायया बहिरिवोद्भूतं यथा निद्रया।
य: साक्षात्कुरुते प्रबोधसमये स्वात्मानमेवाद्वयं
    तस्मै श्रीगुरुमूर्तये नम इदं श्रीदक्षिणामूर्तये ॥

Sri Sankaracharya: Dakshinamurti Stotra, 2.

यस्यैव स्फुरणं सदात्मकमसत्कल्पार्थकं भासते
    साक्षात्तत्त्वमसीति वेदवचसा यो बोधयत्याश्रितान्।
यत्साक्षात्करणाद्भवेन्न पुनरावृत्तिर्भवाम्भोनिधौ
    तस्मै श्रीगुरुमूर्तये नम इदं श्रीदक्षिणामूर्तये ॥

Dakshinamurti Stotra, 4.

223.   I offer my salutations to that beneficent Being who is incarnate as the
preceptor (Guru).   He, the Atman, appearing as the individual soul through the power
of ignorance, sees (in the waking state)—
as one does in sleep—the universe, which
in reality exists within Himself, as something external, like a city seen reflected in
a mirror.   But in His enlightened state He
realises His own Self, the One without a
second.

224.   I offer my salutations to the beneficent Being who is incarnate in the preceptor (Guru), the light of whose absolute
existence shines forth in the world of appear-
ance, who instructs the disciples with the
holy text, ' That Thou art ', realising
whom the soul never more returns to the
ocean of birth and death.

12

परात्मानमेकं जगद्बीजमाद्यं

निरीहं निराकारमोङ्कारवेद्यम् ।

यतो जायते पाल्यते येन विश्वं

तमीशं भजे लीयते यत्र विश्वम् ॥ २२५ ॥

Sri Sankaracharya : Vedasarasivastava, 5.

अजं शाश्वतं कारणं कारणानां

शिवं केवलं भासकं भासकानाम् ।

तुरीयं तम:पारमाद्यन्तहीनं

प्रपद्ये परं पावनं द्वैतहीनम् ॥ २२६ ॥

Vedasarasivastava, 7.

नमस्ते नमस्ते विभो विश्वमूर्ते

नमस्ते नमस्ते चिदानन्दमूर्ते ।

नमस्ते नमस्ते तपोयोगगम्य

नमस्ते नमस्ते श्रुतिज्ञानगम्य ॥ २२७ ॥

Vedasarasivastava, 8.

225. I adore the Lord, the supreme Self, the One, the primordial seed of the universe, the desireless and the formless, who is realised through the divine mystic symbol Om, from whom the universe comes into being, by whom it is sustained, and into whom it dissolves.

226. I take refuge in Him, the unborn, the eternal, the cause of all causes, the good, the absolute, the light of lights, the transcendental, the one beyond darkness, without beginning and end, the supreme purifier, devoid of all duality.

227. Salutations to Thee, O all-pervading Being who appearest in the form of the universe. Salutations to Thee, who art of the form of knowledge and bliss. Salutations to Thee, who art attained through disciplines and meditation. Salutations to Thee, who art realised by the highest knowledge revealed in the scriptures.

आयुर्नश्यति पश्यतां प्रतिदिनं याति क्षयं यौवनं

प्रत्यायान्ति गताः पुनर्न दिवसाः कालो जगद्भक्षकः ।

लक्ष्मीस्तोयतरङ्गभङ्गचपला विद्युच्चलं जीवितं

तस्मान्मां शरणागतं शरणद त्वं रक्ष रक्षाधुना ॥

Sivaparadha-kshamapana-stotra, 13.

करचरणकृतं वाक्कायजं कर्मजं व।

श्रवणनयनजं वा मानसं वाऽपराधम् ।

विहितमविहितं वा सर्वमेतत्क्षमस्व

जय जय करुणाब्धे श्रीमहादेव शम्भो ॥२२९॥

Sivaparadha-kshamapana-stotra, 14.

त्वदन्यः शरण्यः प्रपन्नस्य नेति

प्रसीद स्मरन्नेव हन्यास्तु दैन्यम् ।

न चेत् ते भवेद्भक्तवात्सल्यहानि-

स्ततो मे दयालो दयां सन्निधेहि ॥ २३० ॥

Siva-bhujanga-prayata-stotra, 10.

228. O Lord, with the passing of every day the duration of life is seen to shorten and youth to decay. The days that are gone do never come back. Verily, time is the devourer of the world. Fortune is as fickle and short-lived as ripples on the surface of water, while life is momentary like the flash of lightning. Therefore, O Thou refuge of all, do Thou even now protect me who seek refuge in Thee.

229. Do Thou forgive me, O Lord, for all my sins committed with my hands, feet, speech, body, ears, eyes and mind, while doing actions enjoined or otherwise. Glory unto Thee, O Thou Lord beneficent, Thou God of gods, Thou ocean of mercy.

230. To the distressed there is no other refuge but Thee. Lord, be propitious. Being remembered, Thou promptly removest the misery of the devotees. Else Thou wilt lose Thy reputation of being gracious towards Thy devotees. Therefore, O Thou merciful Lord, have mercy on me.

अयं दानकालस्त्वहं दानपात्रं
भवान्नाथ दाता त्वदन्यं न याचे ।
भवद्भक्तिमेव स्थिरां देहि मह्यं
कृपाशील शम्भो कृतार्थोऽस्मि तस्मात् ॥२३१॥

Siva-bhujanga-prayata-stotra, 11.

असारे संसारे निजभजनदूरे जडधिया
भ्रमन्तं मामन्धं परमकृपया पातुमुचितम् ।
मदन्य: को दीनस्तव कृपणरक्षातिनिपुण-
स्त्वदन्य: को वा मे त्रिजगति शरण्य: पशुपते ॥

Sri Sankaracharya : Sivanandalahari, 13.

231. This is the proper time for making gifts. Lord, I am a fit recipient, Thou art a great giver, and none else but Thee shall I approach for begging. Grant me but unflinching devotion unto Thee. O benign Lord, with that alone shall I deem my life's goal attained.

232. O Lord, with a dull intellect and imperfect insight I whirl in this unsubstantial world of births and deaths, uncongenial to the practice of devotion. Thou shouldst in Thy infinite mercy save me. Is there a creature more miserable than myself ? And is there anyone more skilled than Thyself in saving the miserable ? Therefore, in the three worlds, who but Thee shall be my saviour ?

प्रभुस्त्वं दीनानां खलु परमबन्धुः पशुपते
प्रमुख्योऽहं तेषामपि किमुत बन्धुत्वमनयोः ।
त्वयैव क्षन्तव्याः शिव मदपराधाश्च सकलाः
प्रयत्नात् कर्तव्यं मदवनमियं बन्धुसरणिः॥२३३॥

Sivanandalahari, 14.

त्वत्पादाम्बुजमर्चयामि परमं त्वां चिन्तयाम्यन्वहं
स्वामीशं शरणं व्रजामि वचसा त्वामेव याचे विभो ।
वीक्षां मे दिश चाक्षुषीं सकरुणां दिव्यैश्चिरं प्रार्थितां
शम्भो लोकगुरो मदीयमनसः सौख्योपदेशं कुरु ॥

Sivanandalahari, 29.

233. Thou art verily the master and the greatest friend of the distressed, while I am the foremost amongst them all. What else is required to establish a relation between us ? O blessed Lord, Thou shouldst forgive all my sins, and bring about my salvation by Thy own earnest effort ; for such is the way of friends.

234. O beneficent preceptor of the universe, I offer worship unto Thy lotus feet and contemplate daily on Thy supreme Self. I surrender myself unto Thee and with my words supplicate Thee. Pray, vouchsafe unto me a gracious glance long sought after even by the gods, and do Thou instruct me in the methods of attaining tranquillity of mind.

योगक्षेममधुरन्धरस्य सकलश्रेयःप्रदोद्योगिनो
दृष्टादृष्टमतोपदेशकृतिनो बाह्यान्तरव्यापिनः ।
सर्वज्ञस्य दयाकरस्य भवतः किं वेदितव्यं मया
शम्भो त्वं परमान्तरङ्ग इति मे चित्ते स्मराम्यन्वहम् ॥

Sivanandalahari, 35.

आत्मा त्वं गिरिजा मतिः सहचराः प्राणाः शरीरं गृहं
पूजा ते विषयोपभोगरचना निद्रा समाधिस्थितिः ।
संचारः पदयोः प्रदक्षिणविधिः स्तोत्राणि सर्वा गिरो
यद्यत्कर्म करोमि तत्तदखिलं शम्भो तवाराधनम् ॥

Sri Sankaracharya : Siva-manasa-puja, 4.

235. O blissful Lord, Thou lookest after the needs of all. Thou art ever intent on promoting our welfare. Nay, Thou dost Thyself instruct us in attaining bliss in this world as well as in the next. Thy presence is felt inside and outside. Thou art both omniscient and gracious. Need I therefore ask aught of Thee ? Let me simply meditate on Thee every day as the inmost essence of all.

236. O Lord, my Self Thou art. My mind I liken to the divine Mother (Thy consort), my vital airs to Thy followers, and my body to Thy temple. My enjoyments I regard as offerings made unto Thee. My sleep is a form of absorption in Thee. My wanderings are like circumambulations while my words are prayers offered unto Thee. O Lord beneficent, whatsoever I do, may it all be as worship made unto Thee.

अविनयमपनय विष्णो
दमय मनः शमय विषयमृगतृष्णाम् ।
भूतदयां विस्ताराय
तारय संसारसागरतः ॥ २३७ ॥

Sri Sankaracharya : Shatpadistotra, 1.

सत्यपि भेदापगमे
नाथ तवाहं न मामकीनस्त्वम् ।
सामुद्रो हि तरङ्गः
कचन समुद्रो न तारङ्गः ॥ २३८ ॥

Shatpadistotra, 2.

यं ब्रह्मारूयं देवमनन्यं परिपूर्णं
हृत्स्थं भक्तैर्लभ्यमजं सूक्ष्ममतर्क्यम् ।
ध्यात्वाऽऽत्मस्थं ब्रह्मविदो यं विदुरीशं
तं संसारध्वान्तविनाशं हरिमीडे ॥ २३९ ॥

Sri Sankaracharya : Harim-ide-stotra, 7.

237. O Thou Lord all-pervading, do Thou remove my egoism and calm my mind. Do Thou take away from me the illusion of the world. Do Thou increase my love for all beings, and save me from the ocean of worldly existence.

238. It is the waves that merge themselves in the ocean, and not the ocean in the waves. So, verily, O Lord, when all differences are removed, it is I that become absorbed in Thee, and not Thou in me.

239. I sing the glory of the Lord who removes the world-ignorance; who is called Brahman, the effulgent being, the One without a second, the all-pervading, indwelling Spirit attained by the devotees; who is unborn, subtle, beyond all reasoning; whom the knowers of Brahman realise in themselves through meditation.

न जानामि दानं न च ध्यानयोगं
न जानामि तन्त्रं न च स्तोत्रमन्त्रम् ।
न जानामि पूजां न च न्यासयोगं
गतिस्त्वं गतिस्त्वं त्वमेका भवानि ॥ २४० ॥

Bhavanyashtaka-stotra.

न जानामि पुण्यं न जानामि तीर्थं
न जानामि मुक्तिं लयं वा कदाचित् ।
न जानामि भक्तिं व्रतं वापि मात-
र्गतिस्त्वं गतिस्त्वं त्वमेका भवानि ॥ २४१ ॥

Bhavanyashtaka-stotra.

विनोदाय चैतन्यमेकं विभज्य
द्विधा देवि जीवः शिवश्चेति नाम्ना ।
शिवस्यापि जीवत्वमापादयन्ती
पुनर्जीवमेनं शिवं वा करोषि ॥ २४२ ॥

Sri San. : Devi-bhujanga-prayata-stotra, 4.

240.   O Mother, I have made no charity;
I have done no meditation; I have observed
no rituals; nor have I uttered any prayer
or holy name. I have performed no
worship; nor have I purified myself through
proper invocations. Therefore, O Thou
Mother of the universe, Thou art my only
refuge; Thou art my only refuge.

241.   O Mother, pious deeds and pilgri-
mages to holy places, I have performed
none. I have never yearned after salvation,
nor aspired to get merged in the Divine.
I possess no devotion, nor have I observed
any vows even. Therefore, O Thou Mother
of the universe, Thou art my only refuge;
Thou art my only refuge.

242.   O Mother, out of sport Thou hast
divided the one absolute Intelligence into
two—soul and God. Having transformed
God into the individual soul, Thou dost
convert that same soul back into God.

कदा वा हृषीकाणि साम्यं भजेयु:

कदा वा न शुत्रुने मित्रं भवानि ।

कदा वा दुराशाविषूचीविलोप:

कदा वा मनो मे समूलं विनश्येत् ॥ २४३ ॥

Devi-bhujanga-prayata-stotra, 19.

जगज्जालमेतत्त्वयैवाम्ब सृष्टं

त्वमेवाद्य यासीन्द्रियैरर्थजालम् ।

त्वमेकैव कर्त्री त्वमेकैव भोक्त्री

न मे पुण्यपापे न मे बन्धमोक्षौ ॥ २४४ ॥

Devi-bhujanga-prayata-stotra, 27.

विधात्री धर्माणां त्वमसि सकलाम्नायजननी

त्वमर्थानां मूलं धनदनमनीयाङ्घ्रिकमले ।

त्वमादि: कामानां जननि कृतकन्दर्पविजये

सतां भक्तेर्बीजं त्वमसि परमब्रह्ममहीषी ॥ २४५ ॥

Sri Sankaracharya, Anandalahari, 8.

243. O Mother of the universe, when will my senses become controlled ? when shall I have neither enemies nor friends ? when shall I be completely free from false and deluding hopes ? when will my false mind be destroyed with its roots ?

244. Mother, Thou hast created this illusion of the world. Thou again art coming in contact with diverse objects through the medium of the senses. Thou art the only doer ; Thou art the only enjoyer ; not I. There is no merit nor demerit, no bondage nor freedom for me.

245. Thou art the ordainer of all scriptures and the regulator of all religious paths and righteousness. Thou art the source of all wealth, and Thy lotus feet are worshipped even by the lord of wealth. O Mother, Thou art the primal cause of all desires. Thou again hast conquered all the passions. Thou art the cause of the devotion of the good. Thou verily art the Consort and the Power of the Supreme Brahman.

13

अयः स्पर्शे लभ्रं सपदि लभते हेमपदवीं

    यथा रथ्यापाथः शुचि भवति गङ्गौघमिलितम् ।

तथा तत्तत्पापैरतिमलिनमन्तर्मम यदि

    त्वयि प्रेम्णा सक्तं कथमिव न जायेत विमलम् ॥

Anandalahari, 12.

न मन्त्रं नो यन्त्रं तदपि च न जाते स्तुतिमहो

    न चाह्वानं ध्यानं तदपि च न जाने स्तुतिकथाः ।

न जाने मुद्रास्ते तदपि च न जाने विलपनं

    परं जाने मातस्त्वदनुसरणं क्लेशहरणम् ॥ २४७ ॥

Devyaparadha-kshamapana-stotra, 1.

पृथिव्यां पुत्रास्ते जननि बहवः सन्ति सरलाः

    परं तेषां मध्ये विरलतरलोऽहं तव सुतः ।

मदीयोऽयं त्यागः समुचितमिदं नो तव शिवे

    कुपुत्रो जायेत क्वचिदपि कुमाता न भवति ॥

Devyaparadha-kshamapana-stotra.

246. Iron touched by the philosopher's stone is transformed into gold. The waters of the road being mixed witn those of the Ganges become pure. In like manner, O Mother, being attached through devotion to Thee, will not my heart become pure, greatly soiled though it be by many sins ?

247. I do not know Thy sacred names nor the symbolic figures for Thy worship. Alas ! I know not how to sing Thy glory, nor how to invoke and meditate upon Thee. I know not words of prayer, nor the diverse rituals of worship, nor how to lay my grief before Thee. But, O Mother, this much I know : that to follow Thee is to remove all my sufferings.

248. O Mother, in this world, in the midst of Thy numerous worthy sons, I happen to be a rare specimen of wantonness. Yet, O Thou beneficent one, it is not proper for Thee to have abandoned me, Thy child. For a bad son may sometimes be born, but never has there been a bad mother.

न मोक्षस्याकाङ्क्षा न च विभववाञ्छापि हृदि मे
न विज्ञानापेक्षा शशिमुखि सुखेच्छापि न पुनः ।
अतस्त्वां संयाचे जननि जननं यातु मम वै
मृडानी रुद्राणी शिव शिव भवानीति जपतः ॥

Devyaparadha-kshamapana-stotra, 8.

नास्था धर्मे न वसुनिचये नैव कामोपभोगे
यद्भाव्यं तद्भवतु भगवन् पूर्वकर्मानुरूपम् ।
एतत् प्रार्थ्यं मम बहुमतं जन्मजन्मान्तरेऽपि
त्वत्पादाम्भोरुहयुगगता निश्चला भक्तिरस्तु ॥

Kulasekhara : Mukundamala, 7.

दिवि वा भुवि वा ममास्तु वासो
नरके वां नरकान्तक प्रकामम ।
अवधीरितशारदारविन्दौ
चरणौ ते मरणेऽपि चिन्तयामि ॥ २५१ ॥

Mukundamala, 8.

249. No desire have I for liberation, nor any hankering after wealth. Neither do I cherish any yearning for knowledge, nor any desire for happiness. O Mother divine, This only I beg of Thee : May my life pass in reciting the divine names.

250. Lord, I do not care for so-called meritorious acts, neither tor wealth, nor for the enjoyment of the objects of desire. Let that which is inevitable fall to my lot according to my previous Karma. But this much is my cherished desire, that I should be endowed with love unshaken for Thy lotus feet in this life, as well as in lives to come.

251. Let me be placed, O Lord, in heaven, or on earth, or in hell, as it pleaseth Thee. I shall even in death think of Thy holy feet which surpass in beauty the autumnal lotus blossoms.

अपराधसहस्रसङ्कुले पतितं भीमभवार्णवोदरे ।
अगतिं शरणागतं हरे कृपया केवलमात्मसात्कुरु ॥

Mukundamala, 13.

कायेन वाचा मनसेन्द्रियैर्वा
बुद्ध्यात्मना वा प्रकृतेः स्वभावात् ।
करोमि यद्यत् सकलं परस्मै
नारायणायेति समर्पयामि ॥ २५३ ॥

Mukundamala, 15.

यत् कृतं यत् करिष्यामि तत् सर्वं न मया कृतम् ।
त्वया कृतं तु फलभुक्त्वमेव मधुसूदन ॥ २५४ ॥

Mukundamala, 16.

नमो नमो वाङ्मनसातिभूमये
नमो नमो वाङ्मनसैकभूमये ।
नमो नमोऽनन्तमहाविभूतये
नमो नमोऽनन्तदयैकसिन्धवे ॥ २५५ ॥

Sri Yamunacharya : Stotraratna, 21

252. I have committed a thousand faults, and am fallen into the terrible ocean of births and deaths. O Thou Saviour, being helpless, I have taken refuge in Thee. Be pleased to make me Thine own.

253. O Lord, whatever I have done through body, speech, mind, senses, intellect, soul, or unconscious natural impulses—all that I dedicate as an offering unto Thee, the supreme, all-pervading Spirit.

254. What apparently I have done or what I may yet do, is really done by Thee and not by me. O Lord, therefore Thou art the enjoyer, and not I.

255. Salutations unto Thee, O Lord. Thou art the origin of mind and speech, but Thee neither mind nor speech can comprehend. O Lord of eternal and infinite glory, O Thou boundless ocean of mercy, salutations unto Thee.

न धर्मनिष्ठोऽस्मि न चात्मवेदी
न भक्तिमांस्त्वच्चरणारविन्दे ।
अकिञ्चनोऽनन्यगतिः शरण्यं
त्वत्पादमूलं शरणं प्रपद्ये ॥ २५६ ॥

Stotraratna, 22.

उदीर्णसंसारदवाशुशुक्षणिं
क्षणेन निर्वाप्य परां च निर्वृतिम् ।
प्रयच्छति त्वच्चरणारुणाम्बुज-
द्वयानुरागामृतसिन्धुशीकरः ॥ २५७ ॥

Stotraratna, 29.

विलासविक्रान्तपरावरालयं
नमस्यदार्तिक्षपणे कृतक्षणम् ।
धनं मदीयं तव पादपङ्कजं
कदा नु साक्षात्करवाणि चक्षुषा ॥ २५८ ॥

Stotraratna, 30

256. I am not steadfast in the practice of virtue, nor do I know the Self, nor am I devoted to Thy lotus feet. I possess no merit whatsoever, and I have no other refuge but Thee. Therefore, O Lord, do I take shelter at Thy blessed feet.

257. A particle of the ambrosial ocean of love cherished for Thy red lotus feet extinguishes in no time the mighty forest fire of worldly existence with its cycle of births and deaths, and bestows the supreme bliss on Thy devotee.

258. O Lord, when shall I see with my own eyes Thy lotus feet which are my wealth, which readily remove the distress of the worshippers, and which transcend both heaven and earth ?

न मृषा परमार्थमेव मे
श्रृणु विज्ञापनमेकमग्रतः ।
यदि मे न दयिष्यसे ततो
दयनीयस्तव नाथ दुर्लभः ॥ २५९ ॥

Stotraratna, 50.

तदहं त्वट्टे न नाथवान्
मट्टे त्वं दयनीयवान् न च ।
विधिनिर्मितमेतदन्वयं
भगवन् पालय मा स्म जीहपः ॥ २६० ॥

Stotraratna, 51.

न देहं न प्राणान् न च सुखमशेषाभिलषितं
न चात्मानं नान्यत् किमपि तव शेषत्वविभवात् ।
बहिर्भूतं नाथ क्षणमपि सहे यातु शतधा
विनाशं तत्सत्यं मधुमथन विज्ञापनमिदम् ॥२६१॥

Stotraratna, 57.

259. O Lord, first of all do Thou hear my prayer. I am speaking only the truth and not falsehood. Unless Thou bestowest Thy mercy on me, Thou wilt never get one more deserving than myself.

260. Therefore, none but Thyself can be a suitable master for me, and none but myself a fit recipient of Thy grace. It is the decree of Providence that Thou shouldst be my master, and I, Thy servant. Do Thou maintain, and never abandon, this relationship.

261. My Lord, this is my sincere prayer to Thee : I do not care for comfort of body, nor for long life, nor for enjoyments so much hankered after by all. I do not want even the knowledge of the Self, nor anything else even for a single moment if they are not to be in Thy association and in Thy service. Let all these then break into a hundred shreds and be destroyed.

दुरन्तस्यानादेरपरिहरणीयस्य महतो
निहीनाचारोऽहं नृपशुरशुभस्यास्पदमपि ।
दयासिन्धो बन्धो निरवधिकवात्सल्यजलधे
तव स्मारं स्मारं गुणगणमितीच्छामि गतभीः ॥

Stotraratna, 58.

पिता त्वं माता त्वं दयिततनयस्त्वं प्रियसुहृत्
त्वमेव त्वं मित्रं गुरुरसि गतिश्चासि जगताम् ।
त्वदीयस्त्वद्भृत्यस्तव परिजनस्त्वद्गतिरहं
प्रपन्नश्चैवं सत्यहमपि तवैवास्मि हि भरः ॥२६३॥

Stotraratna, 60.

262. O Thou the friend of the help-less, Thou boundless ocean of compassion and love divine, I am the seat of infinite evils, hard to remove, beginningless and irresistible. Devoid of all moral discipline, I am a veritable, beast among men. But, my Lord, remembering the infinitude of Thy mercy again and again, I have become fearless. So do I place this humble prayer before Thee.

263. Thou art the father, mother, husband and son. Thou art the dear friend, relative and teacher, and the goal of the universe. I am Thine own, Thy servant and attendant ; Thou art my only refuge. I have taken shelter in Thee, and verily, O Lord, does my burden rest wholly on Thee.

न वै याचे राज्यं न च कनकमाणिक्यविभवं
    न याचेऽहं रम्यां सकलजनकाम्यां वरवधूम् ।
सदा काले काले प्रमथपतिना गीतचरितो
    जगन्नाथस्वामी नयनपथगामी भवतु मे ॥ २६४ ॥

Sri Chaitanya : Jagannathashtaka, 7.

हर त्वं संसारं द्रुततरमसारं सुरपते
    हर त्वं पापानां विततिमपरां यादवपते ।
अहो दीनेऽनाथे निहितमचलं निश्चितपदं
    जगन्नाथस्वामी नयनपथगामी भवतु मे ॥२६५॥

Jagannathashtaka, 8.

न धनं न जनं न सुन्दरीं
    कविता वा जगदीश कामये ।
मम जन्मनि जन्मनीश्वरे
    भवताद्भक्तिरहैतुकी त्वयि ॥ २६६ ॥

Sri Chaitanya : Sikshashtaka, 4.

264-265. O Lord, I do not beg for a kingdom, nor for gold and jewels. Nor do I ask for a beautiful bride, so eagerly desired by men. Do Thou reveal Thyself unto me, O mighty Lord of the universe, whose glory is always sung even by the greatest of gods. O God of gods, pray, remove forthwith from my mind all fascination for this vain and fleeting world. Lord, take away the heaps of heinous sins from me. O God, Thou ever bestoweth Thy unfailing mercy upon the miserable and the helpless. O mighty Lord of the universe, do Thou reveal Thyself unto me.

266. O Lord of the universe, I want neither wealth nor attendants, neither a beautiful wife nor intellectual attainments. Do Thou grant that I may be blessed in every birth with selfless devotion to Thee, O Lord.

यन्मायावशवर्ति विश्वमखिलं ब्रह्मादिदेवाः सुराः
यत्सत्त्वादमृषैव भाति सकलं रज्जौ यथाहेर्भ्रमः ।
यत्पादं प्लवमेव भाति हि भवाम्भोधेस्तितीर्षावतां
वन्देऽहं तमशेषकारणपरं रामाख्यमीशं हरिम् ॥

Sri Tulasidas : Ramayana, I, 6.

नान्या स्पृहा रघुपते हृदयेऽस्मदीये
सत्यं वदामि च भवानखिलान्तरात्मा ।
भक्तिं प्रयच्छ रघुपुङ्गव निर्भरां मे
कामादिदोषरहितं कुरु मानसं च ॥ २६८ ॥

Tulasidas : Ramayana, V, 2.

267. I salute the Lord, the remover of sin, who is called Rama; who is beyond the ultimate cause; by whose Maya is controlled the entire universe as well as the hosts of gods beginning from the creator; because of whose existence everything appears real like the illusory perception of a snake on a rope; and whose feet are like a raft to those who desire to cross the ocean of life.

268. O Lord, O Thou the inmost Self of all, I tell Thee the truth: I do not cherish any worldly desire in my heart. Do Thou grant me intense devotion unto Thee. Do Thou also free my mind from passions and other impurities.

14

नमामि भक्तवत्सलं कृपालुशीलकोमलं

भजामि ते पदाम्बुजं अकामिनां स्वधामदम् ।

तदेकमद्भुतं प्रभुं निरीहमीश्वरं विभुं

जगद्गुरुञ्च शाश्वतं तुरीयमेककेवलम् ॥ २६९ ॥

Tulasidas : Ramayana, III, Ramastotra, 1.

भजामि भाववल्लभं कुयोगिनां सुदुर्लभं

स्वभक्तकल्पपादपं समस्तसेव्यमन्वहम् ।

अरूपरूपभूपतिं नतोऽहमुर्विबीजापतिं

प्रसीद देहि मे विभो पदाब्जभक्तिमाशु ते ॥

Tulasidas : Ramayana, III, Ramastotra, 10.

नमामीशमीशाननिर्वाणरूपं

विभुं व्यापकं ब्रह्मवेदस्वरूपम् ।

अजं निर्गुणं निर्विकल्पं निरीहं

चिदाकारमाकाशवासं भजेऽहम् ॥ १७१ ॥

Tulasidas : Ramayana, VII, Sivashtaka, 1.

269. O Lord, I bow to Thee, who art compassionate, gracious and sweet. Thou alone, O Lord, art marvellous, selfless, mighty and omnipresent. Thou art the teacher of the world, eternal, transcendent, one and absolute. I worship Thy lotus feet that enable the selfless souls to attain to Thy eternal abode.

270. I offer worship unto Thee, O Lord of love, whom the worldly-minded cannot reach, but who art to the devotees the wish-yielding tree, and the object of worship to all. Lord of the universe, Thou art formless and yet with forms. Have mercy upon me, O Lord, and pray, promptly grant me devotion to Thy lotus feet.

271. Salutations unto Thee, thou all-pervading and great Lord. Thou art liberation itself, and the revealed scripture is Thy embodied form. I worship Thee, the unborn, attributeless and unconditioned one. Thou art without any desire. Intelligence itself is Thy nature, and the sky Thy garment.

कलातीतकल्याणकल्पान्तकारिन्

सदा सज्जनानन्ददातः पुरारे ।

चिदानन्दसन्दोह मोहापकारिन्

प्रसीद प्रसीद प्रभो मन्मथारे ॥ २७२ ॥

Tulasidas : Ramayana, VII, Sivashtaka, 6.

न यावद्द्वानीशपादारविन्दं

भजन्तीह लोके चतुर्वर्गकामाः ।

न तावलभन्ते भवे शान्तिलेशं

प्रसीद प्रभो सर्वभूताधिवास ॥ २७३ ॥

Tulasidas : Ramayana, VII, Sivashtaka, 7.

न जानामि योगं जपं नैव पूजां

नतोऽहं सदा सर्वतः शर्वे तुभ्यम् ।

जराजन्मदुःखौघतातप्यमानं

प्रभो पाहि पापान्मामीश शम्भो ॥ २७४ ॥

Tulasidas : Ramayana, VII, Sivashtaka, 8.

272. O Lord, Thou art beyond all duality, the cause of absolute good and also of cosmic dissolution. Thou art the bestower of bliss on the holy ones. Thou art the embodiment of knowledge, and the remover of delusion. Be Thou propitious unto me, O destroyer of passion.

273. Those that aspire in this world after the fourfold object of life,—virtue, wealth, enjoyment and salvation—can hardly be the recipients of peace supreme, unless, O Lord divine, they worship Thy lotus feet. Be Thou propitious unto me, O Thou the abode of all beings.

274. I do not know the practice of Yoga, nor how to repeat Thy holy name. Neither do I know any form of worship. I am Thy humble suppliant, sorely afflicted with the countless miseries of birth and old age. Do Thou save me from sins. To Thee, O Lord, I offer my salutations.

सम्पादयन्त्यविरतं त्वविरामवृत्ता
    या वै स्थिता कृतफलं त्वकृतस्य नेत्री ।
सा मे भवत्वनुदिनं वरदा भवानी
    जानाम्यहं ध्रुवमिदं धृतकर्मपाशा ॥ २७५ ॥

Swami Vivekananda : Ambastotra, 2

मित्रे शत्रौ त्वविषमं तव पद्मनेत्रं
    स्वस्थे दुःस्थे त्ववितथस्तव हस्तपातः ।
छाया मृतेस्तव दया त्वमृतश्च मात-
    र्मुञ्चन्तु मा न परमे शुभदृष्टयस्ते ॥ २७६ ॥

Ambastotra, 5

काम्बा शिवा क गृणनं मम हीनबुद्धेः
    दोर्भ्यां विधर्तुमिव यामि जगद्विधात्रीम् ।
चिन्त्यं श्रिया सुचरणं त्वभयप्रतिष्ठं
    सेवापरैरभिनुतं शरणं प्रपद्ये ॥ २७७ ॥

Ambastotra, 6.

275. May the Mother of the universe, whose activity knows no pause—incessantly distributing the fruits of actions done, guiding unceasingly all actions yet to come—bestow Her boon of blessing on me, Her child for ever more. I realise, I know, that it is She who holds the ropes of Karma in Her hands.

276. On friend and foe Thy lotus eyes fall alike. Ever Thine animating touch brings fruit equally to the fortunate and the unfortunate. The shade of death and immortality,—both these, O Mother, are Thy grace. O Mother supreme, may Thy gracious face be never turned away from me, Thy child.

277. Where art Thou, O Mother, and where my words of praise? My understanding is so poor. It is like the desire to seize with my puny hands the sole supporter of the universe! So at Thy blessed feet, which are contemplated by the Goddess of Fortune Herself, which form the abode of fearlessness, which are worshipped by those devoted to service true, do I take refuge.

निखिलभुवनजन्मस्थेमभङ्गप्ररोहाः

अकलितमहिमानः कल्पिता यत्र तस्मिन् ।

सुविमलगगनामे ईशंसंस्थेऽप्यनीशे

मम भवतु भवेऽस्मिन्भासुरो भाववन्धः ॥ २७८ ॥

Swami Vivekananda : Sivastotra, 1.

गलिततिमिरमालः शुभ्रतेजः प्रकाशः

धवलकमलशोभः ज्ञानपुञ्जाट्टहासः ।

यमिजनहृदिगम्यः निष्कलो ध्यायमानः

प्रणतमवतु मां सः मानसो राजहंसः ॥ २७९ ॥

Sivastotra, 5.

278. Salutation to the Lord beneficent, whose glory is immeasurable, who resembles the sky in purity, to whom are attributed the phenomena of creation, preservation and dissolution of the universe. May the burning devotion of this, my life, get attached to Him, who, while being Lord of all, remains subject to none.

279. From whom all gloom and darkness have dispersed; who is like the radiant light, white, beautiful, as is the bloom of a white lotus; whose loud laughter sheds luminous knowledge; whose absolute nature is by meditation realised in the self-controlled heart;—may that lordly Swan of the lake of my mind guard me, lying prostrate before Him.

नरदेव देव　　　　　　　जय जय नरदेव
शक्तिसमुद्रसमुत्थतरङ्गम् ।
दर्शितप्रेमविजृम्भितरङ्गम् ॥
संशयराक्षसनाशमहास्त्रम् ।
यामि गुरुं शरणं भववैद्यम् ॥ २८० ॥
नरदेव देव　　　　　　　जय जय नरदेव

Swami Vivekananda : Gurustotra.

नरदेव देव　　　　　　　जय जय नरदेव
अद्वयतत्त्वसमाहितचित्तम् ।
प्रोज्ज्वलभक्तिपटावृतवृत्तम् ॥
कर्मकलेबरमद्भुतचेष्टम् ।
यामि गुरुं शरणं भववैद्यम् ॥ २८१ ॥
नरदेव देव　　　　　　　जय जय नरदेव

Swami Vivekananda : Gurustotra.

280. O Lord incarnate, O Lord divine, glory unto Thee. I take refuge in Thee, the divine Master, who art like a wave arising out of the ocean of cosmic energy; who enactest Thy manifold divine play out of love infinite; who art the destroyer of the demon of doubt; who art the divine healer of the disease of worldliness. O Lord incarnate, O Lord divine, glory unto Thee.

281. I take refuge in Thee, who art established in the knowledge of the One without a second; whose life is wrapped in the luminous garment of devotion; whose body is ever active in doing good to mankind; whose deeds are wonderful; who art the divine healer of the disease of worldliness. O Lord incarnate, O Lord divine, glory unto Thee.

UNIVERSAL PRAYERS

MISCELLANEOUS

अजं निर्विकल्पं निराकारमेकं
निरानन्दमानन्दमद्वैतपूर्णम् ।
परं निर्गुणं निर्विशेषं निरीहं
परब्रह्मरूपं गणेशं भजेम ॥ २८२ ॥

Ganesastava, 1.

गुणातीतमानं चिदानन्दरूपं
चिदाभासकं सर्वगं ज्ञानगम्यम् ।
मुनिध्येयमाकाशरूपं परेशं
परब्रह्मरूपं गणेशं भजेम ॥ २८३ ॥

Ganesastava, 2.

जगत्कारणं कारणज्ञानरूपं
सुरादिं सुखादिं गुणेशं गणेशम् ।
जगद्व्यापिनं विश्ववन्द्यं सुरेशं
परब्रह्मरूपं गणेशं भजेम ॥ २८४ ॥

Ganesastava, 3.

282. O Lord, Thou art unborn, absolute and formless; Thou art beyond bliss and again bliss itself—the One and the Infinite. Thou art the supreme, without attributes, differentiation and desire. Thou art verily the supreme Brahman. To Thee, O Lord, do we offer our worship.

283. Thy nature is beyond attributes. Thou art the embodiment of intelligence and bliss, the effulgent Spirit, the all-pervading, the goal of knowledge. Thou art the object of meditation to the sages, formless and omnipresent like ether. Thou art the supreme Lord, the supreme Brahman. To Thee, O Lord, do we offer our worship.

284. Thou art the cause of the world, the primal knowledge, the origin of gods, the origin of bliss, the lord of Gunas, the lord of heavenly hosts. Thou pervadest the universe and art worshipped by all. Thou art the lord of gods, Thou art verily the supreme Brahman. To Thee O Lord, do we offer our worship.

आदिदेव नमस्तुभ्यं प्रसीद मम भास्कर ।
दिवाकर नमस्तुभ्यं प्रभाकर नमोऽस्तु ते ॥ २८५ ॥

Siva : Suryashtaka.

महतः परितः प्रसर्पतस्तमसो दर्शनभेदिनो भिदे ।
दिननाथ इव स्वतेजसा हृदयव्योम्नि मनागुदेहि नः ॥

Upamanyu : Sivastotra, 3.

क दशं विदधामि किं करो-
म्यनुतिष्ठामि कथं भयाकुलः ।
क नु तिष्ठसि रक्ष रक्ष मा-
मयि शम्भो शरणागतोऽस्मि ते ॥ २८७ ॥

Upamanya : Sivastotra, 15.

माता रामो मत्पिता रामचन्द्रः
स्वामी रामो मत्सखा रामचन्द्रः ।
सर्वस्वं मे रामचन्द्रो दयालु-
र्नान्यं जाने नैव जाने न जाने ॥ २८८ ॥

Ramarakshastotra.

285. O Thou primeval Being, Salutation to Thee. O Thou Being resplendent, be gracious unto me. O Thou creator of day, I bow to Thee. O Thou divine illuminator, salutation to Thee.

286. In the darkness that encircles us all round and shuts our vision, do Thou, Lord, just rise like the sun, and dispel it all with Thy light divine.

287. Whither shall I turn? What shall I do? How shall I, oppressed with fear, support myself? Where art Thou, O Lord beneficent? I have taken refuge in Thee. Do Thou save me, save me.

288. The Divine is my mother, the Divine is my father, the Divine is my lord, the Divine is my friend. The Divine, who is merciful, is my all-in-all. I know none else; I know none else; no, not I.

15

भद्रकाल्यै नमो नित्यं सरस्वत्यै नमो नमः ।
वेदवेदाङ्गवेदान्तविद्यास्थानेभ्य एव च ॥ २८९ ॥

Sarasvati Pranama Mantra.

ब्रह्मस्वरूपा परमा ज्योतीरूपा सनातनी ।
सर्वविद्याधिदेवी या तस्यै वाण्यै नमो नमः ॥ १९० ॥

Yajnavalkya : Sarasvatistotra.

यया विना जगत्सर्वं शश्वज्जीवन्मृतं भवेत् ।
ज्ञानाधिदेवी या तस्यै सरस्वत्यै नमो नमः ॥ २९१ ॥

Sarasvatistotra.

यया विना जगत्सर्वं मूकमुन्मत्तवत्सदा ।
या देवी वागधिष्ठात्री तस्यै वाण्यै नमो नमः ॥ २९२ ॥

Sarasvatistotra.

289. Constant salutations to Thee, O Mother beneficent. Thou art the stay of the Veda and the auxiliary branches of the Veda, of the Vedanta and all forms of learning. Salutations to Thee, O Thou Goddess of learning.

290. O Mother, Thou art the personification of Brahman. Thou art the supreme Spirit, the Light divine, the eternal Being. Thou art the presiding deity of all branches of learning. Salutations to Thee, O Goddess of speech.

291. But for Thee the whole world would appear lifeless. Thou art the presiding deity of knowledge. Salutations to Thee, O Goddess of learning.

292. But for Thee the whole world would appear dumb and demented. Thou art the presiding deity of speech. Salutations to Thee, O Mother, O Goddess of speech.

ऐं ऐं ऐं इष्टमन्त्रे कमलभव-

मुखाम्भोजभूतिस्वरूपे

रूपारूपप्रकाशे सकलगुण-

मये निर्गुणे निर्विकारे ।

न स्थूले नैव सूक्ष्मेऽप्यविदित-

विभवे नापि विज्ञानतत्त्वे

विश्वे विश्वान्तरात्मे सुरवरनमिते

निष्कले नित्यशुद्धे ॥ २९३ ॥

Brahma : Sarasvatistotra.

ह्रीं ह्रीं ह्रीं जापतुष्टे हिमरुचि-

मुकुटे वल्लकीव्यग्रहस्ते

मातर्मातर्नमस्ते दह दह

जडतां देहि बुद्धिं प्रशान्ताम् ।

विद्ये वेदान्तवेद्ये परिणत-

पठिते मोक्षदे मुक्तिमार्गे

मार्गातीतस्वरूपे भव मम वरदा

शारदे शुभ्रहारे ॥ २९४ ॥

Brahma : Sarasvatistotra.

293. O Mother, Thou revealest both the form and the formless. Thou art the embodiment of all attributes. Thou, again, art without attributes and change. Thou art neither gross nor subtle, and Thy glory is incomprehensible. Thou art beyond knowledge. Thou art everything, the inmost self of everything, the object of adoration even to the chief of gods. Thou art indivisible and eternally pure.

294. O Mother, Thou art knowledge supreme. Thou art known through the highest revelation and Thy glory is recited by the perfect ones. Thou art the giver of salvation, Thou art the way to salvation, but yet dost transcend it. Be propitious unto me, O Thou Goddess of learning. Be pleased to remove my dullness, and endow me with a keen and tranquil understanding.

आधारभूते चाभेये धृतिरूपे धुरन्धरे ।
ध्रुवे ध्रुवपदे धीरे जगद्धात्रि नमोऽस्तु ते ॥ २९५ ॥

Jagaddhatristava.

जयदे जगदानन्दे जगदेकप्रपूजिते ।
जय सर्वगते दुर्गे जगद्धात्रि नमोऽस्तु ते ॥ २९६ ॥

Jagaddhatristava.

सूक्ष्मातिसूक्ष्मरूपे च प्राणापानादिरूपिणि ।
भावाभावस्वरूपे च जगद्धात्रि नमोऽस्तु ते ॥ २९७ ॥

Jagaddhatristava.

295. O Mother, Thou art the container of all and again the things contained. Thou art the supporter of all, and the bearer of the burden of all. Thou art the eternal Being, the eternal abode and tranquillity embodied. O Thou Protectress of the universe, salutations to Thee.

296. Thou art the giver of success, the bliss of the world, the one object of its adoration. Glory unto Thee. Thou art all-pervading and rescuest men from difficulties. O Thou Protectress of the universe, salutations to Thee.

297. Thou art subtler than the subtlest. Thou art the vital energy in beings. Thou art both existence and non-existence. O Thou Protectress of the universe, salutations to Thee.

अगम्ये जगतामाद्ये माहेश्वरि वराङ्गने ।
अशेषरूपे रूपस्थे जगद्धात्रि नमोऽस्तु ते ॥ २९८ ॥

Jagaddhatristava.

तीर्थेयज्ञतपोदानयोगसारे जगन्मयि ।
त्वमेव सर्वा सर्वेस्था जगद्धात्रि नमोऽस्तु ते ॥ २९९ ॥

Jagaddhatristava.

दयारूपे दयादृष्टे दयार्द्रे दुःखमोचिनि ।
सर्वापत्तारिके दुर्गे जगद्धात्रि नमोऽस्तु ते ॥ ३०० ॥

Jagaddhatristava.

अगम्यधामधामस्थे महायोगीशहृत्पुरे ।
अमेयभावकूटस्थे जगद्धात्रि नमोऽस्तु ते ॥ ३०१ ॥

Jagaddhatristava.

298. Thou art the Being incomprehensible, the cause of the universe, the great divine energy, the goddess supreme. Thou assumest infinite forms and pervadest all forms. O Thou Protectress of the universe, salutations to Thee.

299. Thou art the goal of all pilgrimage and sacrifice, penance, charity and spiritual practice. Thou art everything, and Thou dost permeate everything. O Thou Protectress of the universe, salutations to Thee.

300. Thou art the embodiment of mercy, Thy very look showers mercy. Thy heart is softened by mercy and Thou art the dispeller of misery. Thou art the saviour of all from every harm ; Thou art yet hard to approach. O Thou Protectress of the universe, salutations to Thee.

301. Thou dwellest in the abode inaccessible ; Thou dwellest in the heart of the great Yogis. Thou art the eternal absolute existence. O Thou Protectress of the universe, salutations to Thee.

महेश्वरे वा जगतामधीश्वरे
　　जनार्देने वा जगदन्तरात्मनि ।
न वस्तुभेदप्रतिपत्तिरस्ति मे
　　तथापि भक्तिस्तरुणेन्दुशेखरे ॥ ३०२ ॥

Vairagyashataka.

विधूय क्लेशान्मे कुरु चरणयुग्मं धृतरसं
　　भवत्क्षेत्रप्राप्तौ करमपि च ते पूजनविधौ ।
भवन्मूर्त्यालोके नयनमथ ते पादतुलसी-
　　परिघ्राणे घ्राणं श्रवणमपि ते चारुचरिते ॥ ३०३ ॥

Narayanabhatta : Narayaniya.

प्रभूताधिव्याधिप्रसभचलिते मामकहृदि
　　त्वदीयं तद्रूपं परमरसचिद्रूपमुदियात् ।
उदञ्चद्रोमाञ्चो गलितबहुहर्षाश्रुनिवहो
　　यथा विस्मर्यासं दुरुपशमपीडापरिभवान् ॥ ३०४॥

Narayanabhatta : Narayaniya.

302. I make no difference in substance between Shiva, the supreme Lord of the universe, and Vishnu, its inmost Self. But still may my devotion continue to be directed to the Lord as Shiva.

303. O Lord, remove my afflictions and bless me so that my feet will find delight in visiting places sacred to Thee and my hands in performing Thy worship. Likewise may my eyes find delight in the vision of Thy form, my nose in the sweet odour of the offerings at Thy sacred feet, and my ears in hearing of Thy charming ways.

304. My mind is violently shaken by untold afflictions, mental as well as physical. O Lord, may that form of Thine which is characterised by supreme bliss and knowledge manifest there, so that with my hairs standing on end and my eyes shedding profuse tears of joy, I may forget these afflictions which cannot easily be rooted out.

विष्णुर्वा त्रिपुरान्तको भवतु वा ब्रह्मा सुरेन्द्रोऽथवा
भानुर्वा शशलक्ष्णोऽथ भगवान् बुद्धोऽथ सिद्धोऽथवा।
रागद्वेषविषार्तिमोहरहितः सत्त्वानुकम्पोद्यतो
यः सर्वैः सह संस्कृतो गुणगणैस्तस्मै नमः सर्वदा ॥

देहबुद्ध्या तु दासोऽस्मि जीवबुद्ध्या त्वदंशकः ।
आत्मबुद्ध्या त्वमेवाहमिति मे निश्चिता मतिः ॥३०६॥

श्रीनाथे जानकीनाथे अभेदः परमात्मनि ।
तथापि मम सर्वस्वं रामः कमललोचनः ॥ ३०७ ॥

305. Whether the highest Being is called Vishnu or Shiva, Brahma or Indra, Sun or Moon, Buddha—the Enlightened—or Mahavir—the Perfect—, I always offer my salutations to Him alone who is free from attachment and hatred, worldliness and ignorance, who is endowed with compassion towards all creatures, and is possessed of all noble attributes.

306. O Lord, while I identify myself with the body I am Thy servant. When I consider myself as an individual soul, I am Thy part. And when I look upon myself as the Spirit, I am one with Thee,—this is my firm conviction.

307. I look upon Vishnu and Rama as one and the same, but still may I hold the beautiful Rama to be my all-in-all.

यं शैवाः समुपासते शिव इति ब्रह्मेति वेदान्तिनो
बौद्धा बुद्ध इति प्रमाणपटवः कर्तेति नैयायिकाः ।
अर्हन्नित्यथ जैनशासनरताः कर्मेति मीमांसकाः
सोऽयं नो विदधातु वाञ्छितफलं त्रैलोक्यनाथो हरिः॥

Hanumannataka.

रूपं रूपविवर्जितस्य भवतो ध्यानेन यत्कल्पितं
स्तुत्यानिर्वचनीयताखिलगुरो दूरीकृता यन्मया ।
व्यापित्वञ्च निराकृतं भगवतो यत्तीर्थयात्रादिना
क्षन्तव्यं जगदीश तद्विकलताद्वेषतयं मत्कृतम् ॥

सर्वेस्तरतु दुर्गाणि सर्वो भद्राणि पश्यतु ।
सर्वस्सद्बुद्धिमाप्नोतु सर्वः सर्वत्र नन्दतु ॥ ३१० ॥

308. May the Lord of the universe, the remover of evil, whom the devotees of Shiva worship as Shiva, the Vedantins as Brahman, the Buddhists as Buddha, the followers of the Nyaya Philosophy who are clever in logic as the Agent, those devoted to the Jaina doctrines as Arhat, the ritualists of the Mimamsa school as Karma—grant us all our hearty desires.

309. O Lord, in my meditation I have attributed forms to Thee who art formless. O Thou Teacher of the world, by my hymns I have, as it were, contradicted that Thou art indescribable. By going on pilgrimage I have, as it were, denied Thy omnipresence. O Lord of the universe, pray, forgive me these threefold faults committed by me.

310. May all be freed from dangers. May all realise what is good. May all be actuated by noble thoughts. May all rejoice everywhere.

सर्वे भवन्तु सुखिनः सर्वे सन्तु निरामयाः ।
सर्वे भद्राणि पश्यन्तु मा कश्चिद् दुःखभाग् भवेत् ॥

दुर्जनः सज्जनो भूयात् सज्जनः शान्तिमाप्नुयात् ।
शान्तो मुच्येत बन्धेभ्यो मुक्तश्चान्यान् विमोचयेत् ॥

मूकं करोति वाचालं पङ्गुं लङ्घयते गिरिम् ।
यत्कृपा तमहं वन्दे परमानन्दमाधवम् ॥ ३१३ ॥

स्वस्ति प्रजाभ्यः परिपालयन्तां
     न्याय्येन मार्गेण महीं महीशाः ।
गोब्रह्मणेभ्यः शुभमस्तु नित्यं
     लोकाः समस्ताः सुखिनो भवन्तु ॥ ३१४ ॥

311. May all be happy. May all be free from disease. May all realise what is good. May none be subject to misery.

312. May the wicked become virtuous. May the virtuous attain tranquillity. May the tranquil be free from bonds. May the freed make others free.

313. I salute the all-blissful Lord of auspiciousness, whose compassion makes the mute eloquent and the cripple cross mountains.

314. May good betide all people. May the sovereign rule the earth, following the righteous path. May all beings ever attain what is good. May the worlds be prosperous and happy.

16

काले वर्षतु पर्जन्यः पृथिवी सस्यशालिनी ।
देशोऽयं क्षोभरहितो ब्राह्मणास्सन्तु निर्भयाः ॥ ३१५ ॥

प्रीयतां पुण्डरीकाक्षः सर्वयज्ञेश्वरो हरिः ।
तस्मिंस्तुष्टे जगत्तुष्टं प्रीणिते प्रीणितं जगत् ॥ ३१६ ॥

315. May the clouds pour rain in time. May the earth be blessed with crops. May this our country be free from calamity. May holy men live without fear.

316. May the Lord, the destroyer of sin, the presiding Deity of all sacred activities, be satisfied. For, He being pleased, the whole universe becomes pleased; He being satisfied, the whole universe feels satisfied.

ओं असतो मा सद्गमय ।

तमसो मा ज्योतिर्गमय ।

मृत्योर्माऽमृतं गमय ॥

ओं पूर्णमदः पूर्णमिदं पूर्णात्पूर्णमुदच्यते ।

पूर्णस्य पूर्णमादाय पूर्णमेवावाशिष्यते ॥

ॐ शान्तिः शान्तिः शान्तिः

Om. *From the unreal lead me to the Real.*
From darkness lead me to Light.
From death lead me to Immortality.

Om. *All that is invisible is filled with the*
infinite Brahman. All that is visible
is also permeated by the infinite
Brahman. The whole universe has
come out of the infinite Brahman.
Brahman is infinite although the
whole universe has come out of it.

Om Peace ! Peace ! Peace !

INDEX

To Sanskrit Passages

GENERAL INDEX

(The numbers given here refer to verses and not to pages.)